AN ENGINEER'S GUIDE TO
HAPPINESS:

Establishing the CRITICAL ELEMENTS of
HAPPINESS for a Fabulous Life

DAVID ANDREW

This book is a work of non-fiction. Unless otherwise noted, the author and the publisher make no explicit guarantees as to the accuracy of the information contained in this book and in some cases, names of people and places have been altered to protect their privacy.

Archway Publishing books may be ordered through booksellers or by contacting:

Archway Publishing
1663 Liberty Drive
Bloomington, IN 47403
www.archwaypublishing.com
844-669-3957

Because of the dynamic nature of the Internet, any web addresses or links contained in this book may have changed since publication and may no longer be valid. The views expressed in this work are solely those of the author and do not necessarily reflect the views of the publisher, and the publisher hereby disclaims any responsibility for them.

Any people depicted in stock imagery provided by Getty Images are models, and such images are being used for illustrative purposes only. Certain stock imagery © Getty Images.

ISBN: 978-1-6657-1808-0 (sc)
ISBN: 978-1-6657-1809-7 (e)

Library of Congress Control Number: 2022901477

Print information available on the last page.

Archway Publishing rev. date: 01/28/2022

Contents

Chapter 1   Where to Start 1

Chapter 2   The Single Most Important Decision of Your
Life: Who Will Be Your Lifelong Partner.................... 23

Chapter 3   What Friends Really Mean 46

Chapter 4   Things around You and the Critical Elements to
Happiness 59

Chapter 5   Tools for a Happier Life: How to Create
Amazing Days 79

Chapter 6   How to Reduce the Number of Rough Pebbles
in Your Life and Other Odds and Ends 102

Chapter 7   Some Objective Strengths You'll Need for a
Happier Life 115

Chapter 8   Educating Our Children: Possibly the Most
Important Book *They* Will Ever Write 130

Chapter 9   Health of Your Body.. 151

Chapter 10 Compartmentalization... 160

Chapter 11 Wealth.. 169

Chapter 12 Being Honest with Yourself, and Other Matters
to Consider 176

Chapter 13 An International Movement....................................... 184

Chapter One
Where to Start …

I'M A GUY WHO HAS had to earn every penny I have ever gotten. I now consider this is a good thing in terms of valuing what I have earned, although I definitely did not think struggling to earn money was a good thing when I was younger. I was certainly not thinking of the valuable lesson I was learning when I was thirteen years old and pushing a lawnmower up a hill several times, followed by trying to control its speed when I had to mow a parallel path downhill without slipping. It was a tough way to earn money. That said, I can also imagine that if I was born into a family with wealth and not required to work at a young age, I would quite likely be of different character. But I also hope that that is not true. I have always been a driven and optimistic person; some call it an innate entrepreneurial quality. Today, I know that I am an incredibly fortunate man who remains very optimistic. Why?

I have remained optimistic ever since I figured out the critical elements to happiness thus leading to a fabulous life. If you truly follow them, as I explain them in this book, I am certain you will have a more rewarding life, a more positive outlook, and more happiness. By reading this book I promise you will see things differently in a very positive and helpful way. The critical elements are part of an objective system, versus an emotional and merely subjective system, that provides specific steps to a clearly happier life including objectively evaluating your own behavior.

The objective of me writing this book should be clear in order to benefit you, and everyone you care about, the most. When I use the term *you*, I mean this book can benefit everyone regardless of age, financial status, sex, education, or origin. The objective of this book is to have your life exceed my life in terms of happiness. I could not be more sincere. Just as parents want their children to be happier, to have a better life than they did, that is my desire for you. Imagine how great a world would be if we could objectively have each generation happier than the prior generation. Wow, what a thought. What a goal to achieve. As a person of science, I know of no better way to start that effort than at the beginning. So let's begin.

As an engineer, I like specifics. I have learned to focus on details. I look at things objectively instead of subjectively. I focus on results based on actions. Through this focus and my life experiences, I have developed these critical elements to success and happiness, and that is exactly what I wish to impart to you. Think of this book as an investment. Using relatable, fundamental analogies to convey a point of view is my preferred methodology. In this first instance, I will compare knowledge to money and hence the investment. Financial experts will tell you that time is your best friend when it comes to making your money work for you. Think of knowledge in the same manner. The sooner you gain knowledge, the more you'll benefit in life from that education. One of the critical elements of happiness is to continue to seek knowledge throughout your life, even if just through new experiences. You will find life more rewarding if you can learn to play an instrument, learn a new language, learn to surf, learn how to have a robust garden, learn CPR, or even learn how an electrical circuit works. In the financial world, the term that describes investing early is compound interest. If you invest $10,000 when you're fifty years old, you won't have much in savings if you wish to retire at sixty-two. In fact, you'll have just $22,522 dollars with a 7 percent annual return. But given that exact same compounding interest at the exact same rate of 7 percent annually, you will have $171,443 (that is more than 7 times $22,522) if you had done nothing more than invest that exact same $10,000 at the age of twenty. Well think of learning about the critical elements in the same manner. The sooner you understand the critical elements, the more you will benefit. But let me make something else very clear. This book has almost nothing to do with money except to say that you have to establish a baseline of income and live within your means. I will address some money issues later in this book. But the reason I do not discuss money at great length is because objectively, there is no factual data that correlates happiness and the amount of wealth you attain. That said, the reason I say you must live within your means is because it's pretty hard to have daily happiness, a major goal of this book, if every day you're fighting financial concerns.

Let's stay briefly on the topic of money. You will read in this book that you should never spend a penny of your money based on someone else's perception of you. That means you don't make a purchase simply because you think it will make you look more important or desirable to other people. You should make a purchase based only on how it makes you feel personally and what you need. Simply said, don't try to impress others. The most critical element of the critical elements is to learn to recognize those who truly care for you in life. They are your "core of support" and will likely be with you for most of your life. This book will make clear that there is an incredible difference between those in life who are just acquaintances, those who are friends, and those who are your core support. Thus, it is critical that you learn how to recognize in a very objective manner those who truly love you. It is a very hard lesson in life to trust someone only to have that trusted individual turn against you. It hurts to be betrayed. Because this is so important, I am going to repeat this statement. The most critical element of the critical elements is to learn to recognize those who truly care for you in life. You have to understand that the people who truly care for you in life, and especially those who truly love you (the highest standard), will not be great in number. That is simply a fact. It is not a bad thing. And in fact, your core of support may not be "people" but may be just one person. But wow, what an amazing person he or she is. You will learn that a critical element for a fabulous life is to share it with that person or those people who are your core of support. Your core of support does not care about the value of your car, the value of your home, the designer of your purse, or the type of smart phone you own. They care only about your happiness. Your core support is never jealous of you or envious of you. Could you imagine your mom or dad being jealous of your success? So if you win the lottery, it is a person in your core of support who you absolutely know will be happy for you without any expectation of financial gain for themselves. That is the person you call when you've learned you've won.

That is also the person you would call when you feel in pain. The core of support cares deeply about you. Have you ever asked yourself this simple yet critical and objective question about someone: Does this person really care more about my happiness than their own? And I mean literally. Ask the question out loud when you're alone. A person who is your core support is someone who would actually give you one of their organs. They would immediately drop everything and show up at your door if you said you needed help. A common model for your core of support is your mom or dad. Think of a perfect mom or dad as a model for your core support. It is a person who is truly happy when you get that promotion. It is a person who cries when they know they might not see you for six months. That is the pedestal upon which a core of support person rests. It's a person who, when you ask the question "Does this person really care about my happiness more than they care about their own?" elicits an immediate yes. You will not only know it—you will feel it. A person who will be in your core of support does not receive a fuzzy yes or a maybe answer.

This also means that you will not know if a person is part of your core of support for quite some time. It may take years, and it will likely take challenges between the two of you. One of the characteristics of the core of support is absolute trust, and absolute trust cannot be earned quickly.

It takes time. For example, I have an incredibly kind, accomplished and confident older sister. She is part of my core of support. If she called me and said, "I need your help. Hurry over, and bring a shovel and a bag of lye," I'd be in my car within minutes with a shovel and a bag of lye and no further questions. But I also understand for her to make that call, she feels the same way about me even though we've never talked about it. We just know. That is because I have a lifetime of experiences and knowledge of my older sister. Because she is my sister, I know her true character. I know her strengths and weaknesses just as she knows mine. There is nothing hidden between us. This knowledge took time, and that passage of time provides a measure of trust. That is the pedestal that a "core of support" individual sits upon.

Do you have someone you can call and who can call you? If not, what does that objectively say about you or those you associate with currently in your life? It is the opinion of your core of support that you should value above all others. Let me also be clear that the number of "friends" you have does not mean you have a more sincere or truer core of support. Actually, that is likely quite the opposite. Objectively, there is no link between the number of likes you have on social media and happiness. One can be in a crowd of acquaintances and still feel alone. And there is no correlation between happiness and the number of friends you have. That does not mean that friends are not important. They could be critically important if you don't have a true core of support, and especially if you have not yet found your lifelong partner. I sincerely wish for no one to be alone. But do not confuse someone who is a friend with an individual who is your core of support. And what is perhaps a good measure to know if you are a good person or good friend? You are likely a good person or good friend if people find it difficult to say goodbye when you have to leave.

As I mentioned earlier, friends can form an important role in a happy life. They form an important role because the worst kind of life is one in which you are lonely. That said, your mom should not be your best friend. It is not because she is not amazing. Your best friend should be someone likely in your age group or perhaps someone who has a similar passion. Your mom is not someone you go to a dance club with, just as there are certain movies you don't watch with your mom. Even though friends are important, a person with two hundred online friends is not twice as happy as a person with one hundred online friends. In fact the opposite may be true, and I will address this later in the book. A friend is commonly found because of where you live, where you work, or where you went to school. If you should change jobs or move, that friend may or may not remain the same level of friend, and that is not a bad thing; that is a part of life. Having new acquaintances and forming new friendships can be exciting and rewarding. One of the critical elements of happiness in life is sharing it.

When I find things particularly important, such as the overall objective of this book, I hope you don't mind that I repeat them. I will repeat that the goal or objective of this book is to have your life exceed my life in terms of happiness. I want you to be able to look forward and feel excitement. I also want you to be able to look backward and think that it has been amazing. I ask that you trust me when I say that that is a very high standard to meet. That is my motivation to write this book after many years of people asking me to do so. It is like the gift of a father to a son, a mother to a daughter. Loving parents should always want their children to be happier than them. Notice that I did not say "richer" than them, because as I stated earlier, happiness is not based on the amount of money you have. Unfortunately, my father didn't understand the critical elements. He did not have my life experiences or guidance to teach him those skill sets, and thus he did not consider the benefits of sitting me down to tell me about what he saw as critical elements. And I didn't have enough life experiences to figure out even the beginning of the critical elements until I was in my late twenties, if that early. It's not like I can remember a specific date. I think that my late twenties seems to be about the time when I started to be more objective and change my way of thinking. I needed more life experiences in the real world versus school. I needed more interactions with various groups of people, and I needed to travel to experience totally different cultures. There is a factual statement that you don't know what you don't know. And some of the worst characters you'll meet in life are those who think they know it all. The critical elements are in fact very logical in hindsight once you know all the elements, but they are complex to perform correctly. That is why it takes an entire book to convey all the critical elements. I know you wish you could simply read a short list to understand the critical elements. And in fact, I wish I could present them that way. It would save me the difficult effort of writing this book.

Let me present one such analysis with a simple statement: Most of us feel protected at home. There is a balance between protection and isolation. Too much isolation is a bad thing. Being safe and protected is generally a good thing, but not if that protection does not allow you to understand the world around you. You cannot live in a bubble and get the most out of life. Generally speaking, a person who does not venture out beyond his or her protections, who does not take risk, will not have the best life. You do not start truly experiencing life until you leave home, wherein you are forced to make decisions about your own life. You have to figure it out on your own. And that is why I had to leave home and get out of school before I could begin to understand the world we live in and discover all those elements that make up the critical elements. It also took time to understand what elements are more critical than others. For example, I already noted the core of support is critical to happiness versus being alone in life.

I was one of those kids who raced for the front door to get out of the house. But once I got beyond the proverbial front door, I had to immediately make decisions. Learning how to make decisions is a great thing. Let me give you another analogy to help me make a point. This analogy is about learning how to drive a car. What if you were a teenager, I handed you the keys to a car for your very first experience behind the wheel, and my sole statement or lesson to you, as I opened the driver's door, was "Figure it out"? If you immediately tried to drive any significant distance, you would fail. You would have difficulty understanding all the controls, which in fact are quite limited compared to all the skills you must have to master life. In order to drive a car with proficiently and expertise, you need very specific instructions and practice with those controls. And that was after you likely sat in the car for many years and were able to observe someone operating the car. What if I gave you the keys to a submarine instead of a car? With the car, you were able to observe it being operated by a good driver. What would your first experience operating the submarine look like? Thus, objectively, the less experience you have with something (e.g., operating a submarine), compared to even very limited experience (e.g., observing someone driving a car), the more time it will take you to master.

The question I ask those of us who are adults who drive is, Did you get more instruction in how to drive and operate a car than you did regarding relationships? Has anyone sat you down and spoken to you for hours regarding the critical elements for a happy life? Did you get more instructions regarding how to drive and operate a car than you did in decision-making skills and discussion on how to be genuinely happy in life? As an example, exactly what specific instructions were you given about what to expect in your first relationship? Your parents knew that you inherently were going to have a first love or first crush. Did they tell you in advance about what you were going to feel? Did they tell you when it would likely happen? Did they tell you what would likely happen? Did they prepare you for when it failed? Did they tell you that failing was not a bad thing? Did they teach you that failing is in fact possibly a good thing that you need not be afraid of, and in fact you can plan for failure to learn the most? Did they tell you that no one has ever done everything right the first time?

In this book, you will learn that you will have to overcome failure to gain the most. That means failure is not always a bad thing. For example, the student wrestling athlete that is willing to take the risk and lose in front of all his schoolmates is building strength, agility, confidence and character. Even if he loses he knows he gave his best during the match almost to exhaustion. He will learn that anyone who criticizes the loss is objectively not a friend. Have you been afraid of not doing something, like trying the taste of beer, because you were concerned about what others may think? Have you also been afraid of trying something, like karaoke, because you were concerned about what others may think? You will learn differently in this book. You do not have to be the smartest to accomplish the most. Sometimes you simply have to work longer on the problems that need to be solved. You may have to be the person who works the hardest. Failure is an opportunity to begin again but with more knowledge. A failure is also not always a fault; it may be the best one can do at a certain point in time. The true mistake would be not to try. Think of going to the moon as a goal. Logically speaking, if you are trying to reach a goal such as going to the moon, in many instances you will succeed faster by eliminating all the failures. So actually you want to fail at a faster rate to get to success quicker. In a sense, you can say that you are developing success from failures. Feeling discouraged and experiencing failure are two of the common steppingstones to success. Those who are in your core of support will never discourage you. And those who do discourage you are simply noise for you to ignore. You will learn that failure is something you can plan for. When you experience failure to whatever degree, you will understand that it is merely part of a process that we have all experienced. In a similar vein, another critical element is that preparedness is very beneficial to a happier life. I am also going to repeat this statement. You will learn later in this book that preparedness, like education and practice, is a critical element to happiness in life. I will add that learning to hold a principled position is also very good in life. In fact, President Lincoln was quoted as saying, "I am a slow walker, but I never walk back." That does not mean we don't make mistakes and that we cannot learn. It means that when it comes to your core values, there can be no mistakes. A core value can be respecting one another, honesty, helping the weak, or being respectful. You will learn in this book that it is natural to try to hold on to what you have instead of discovering what is possible. Have you ever been taught to think in decades instead of days as a form of analysis? As an example, just because your home is comfortable for today and tomorrow, is it also the home you want for the next twenty years? What are the variables in the next twenty years? What can you learn by factoring in time? These types of questions and facts will help you with a lot of decisions. Another core element is that when you are planning, you should also always do so in writing. Putting something in writing adds clarity to the endeavor and to the lesson. There is a clear difference between talking about something versus recording it in writing. Again, this is a simple element. We naturally feel prouder about, and thus talk about, our wins, and we do not talk about our losses.

As mentioned earlier, you will see that losses or failures will happen. Having a loss or failure is not a bad thing but is a beginning for something else that can actually be much better. In the same regard, you cannot change the past. The failures or the losses happened. But what if you were prepared for the loss or failure? It is not a question of whether we will face failure; failures and disappointments are a part of life for everyone. The real questions is, How will you choose to react to failure when it comes your way? In fact, you will learn in this book that some of the smartest people actually seek failure as an outcome. Realize that you make a chain stronger by identifying its weakest links. If you're testing a relationship, it is the bad times that test sincerity. It's easy to have a great relationship in the good times when everyone has money, everyone is healthy, and there are no life-changing decisions to be made. How much better would life be if you could be prepared to accept a loss or have knowledge in advance of something bad, instead of being shocked or surprised by it? The more you know, the less you fear. That is a strong lesson.

Similarly, imagine if you or I could speak to every person out there feeling so much pain that they would be considering suicide. Now imagine that you could go back in time, speak to that person in advance, and prepare them in such a manner that you could prevent such feelings. I am suggesting in this book that you can do just that. Understanding the critical elements not only enhances the happiness in your life but also reduces the impact of the bad. I will repeat that. Understanding the critical elements not only enhances the happiness in your life but also reduces the impact of the bad. Learning in advance of what is likely to happen is much better than experiencing something alone or with no knowledge. Let me give you some examples. That is why many businesses, local governments, the military, and even hospitals run drills that model possible events, so folks do not panic when similar events actually happen. Imagine being a firefighter and being told to put out a fire without first experiencing the training that has you experience a fire in a controlled setting. Imagine driving your car suddenly onto ice for the first time without first experiencing a controlled demonstration where you learn how to make controlled maneuvers. How you respond in such a situation could vary widely. The outcomes are totally different. In a similar analogy, the critical elements are a system that will help you to handle extreme situations better by preparing you for life's possible and perhaps likely events. Although this book is actually more focused on helping you to see how amazing life can be, it also recognizes that there will be losses and failures, and thus it establishes a system to soften those life events.

A perfect life is actually about balance. Life is like riding a surfboard: it is most stable when you are moving forward. A great standard to evaluate relationships or activities is whether more involvement would enhance your day and life. If you have a relationship with someone, and that someone brings negativity into your life, you should try to avoid that relationship. But negativity should not be equated with those in need. There are those in need of education, in need of compassion, and in need of supervision, to name a few. Helping those people can be extremely rewarding. What I mean by negativity is someone who takes you off the path you want to follow. Do not get into a car with someone who is an unsafe driver. Do not allow peer pressure to cause you to have "just one more drink." On the opposite side of the coin, also realize that your life will not be as fulfilled if you do not have any challenges. Having a goal, a dream, or an objective is very fulfilling. If you want to live a happy life, keep establishing goals to strive for and to keep you busy. Let me give you an analogy. If you began to play a game, and you easily win each and every time, how long would you remain interested in the game? A week? A month? A year? Part of what makes life exciting is challenges, and hopefully most of those challenges are those that you decide to take on. The challenge to learn the piano, run a marathon, write computer code, surprise your teacher, lose fifty pounds, or do fifty sit-ups a week. I am not saying that a life of constant challenge is good thing. A life of constant challenge is clearly the opposite to a life where you are never challenged. A life where you are never challenged is also not a perfect life. Life is about balance, but it is not an equal balance. You want to experience a vast greater amount of happiness than you do unplanned challenges. Most of us want to see more happiness on a daily basis because life as a whole can be difficult.

Returning to the analogy of learning to drive a car, this book is similar to the learning to drive in that I cannot simply hand you the keys to a car and expect you to know exactly how to operate that car, especially to its full potential. Even if you had committed to memory the owner's manual of a car, it doesn't mean you will know how to drive it. This book is a manual, a list of the critical elements, to operating your life to its full potential by not only avoiding the crashes but also accelerating to the finish line that you can't even see. If someone asks me if I am excited about the future, my resolute answer is an emphatic yes. And that is not a subjective answer. It is a very objective answer. I can give many specifics and details as to why I am excited about my future. Because it is the future, it is based only on possibilities. That means I am objectively excited about all the possibilities. Just as a professional engineer can prove to you the proper operation of a system, once you finish this book, if I have conveyed the critical elements correctly, you will be able to maximize your happiness. I can list for you many things that I am looking forward to experiencing, so much so that I constantly mention to my amazingly wonderful wife that I wish I could slow down time. As a side note, I also wish that once in my life, someone would tell me that I was annoyingly brilliant LOL!

I feel I don't have enough time left, and yet I expect to live for several more decades. That is how many things I am still excited to do. That is also my wish for you: that you will be so excited with life that you'll want to slow it down. If someone asked me if I have had a great life thus far, I would reply yes. Have I had rough patches and failures? Absolutely. But they are in my past. I can also list the things that have made me very fortunate in life thus far. Similarly, I wish that you have an answer when someone asks you at some party or gathering if you had a great past month or year, and why. In fact, I hope you will have a long list of answers.

Feeling the need to slow down life is a very good thing. I can give you an analogy of two totally different vacations. The first type of vacation is one where you planned to see ten different locations within a seven-day period. The second type of vacation is where you have a list of ten different possible locations, and you prioritize three within a seven-day period. Which of the two vacations is more relaxing and arguably more rewarding? The lessons from this book conclude that the second type of vacation is more rewarding because the main objective of a vacation is relaxation and not merely seeing a large quantity of locations. Besides, the first three locations you prioritize likely help you in deciding whether you want to return to the area to see the other seven—and if so, that vacation area will be added to the list of things that you're looking forward to experiencing. You'll be approaching that future vacation with a better education of the area so your next visit can be that much better. It's fabulous to look forward to things in life.

As an engineer, the way I am approaching this book is to focus on the tools that will allow you to be excited about the future. I choose the word *allow* because it is all up to you. In simple terms, life is all about time and how you choose to use that time. One of the building blocks of time is a day. Just as I would approach an engineering problem with a unit of measure, I chose to formulate the critical elements to be most focused on a day. The goal is to have as many amazing days in the future as possible. A day is a simple measure of time that we all understand. I have designed this book to provide you with the tools to increase your joy in each given day. The benefit of having the timeline limited to a day is that it allows you to measure a degree of happiness before you start all over again. In other words, a goal is to learn from past days and to exceed happiness in future days. When you have a bad day, which is a part of life, it will end, and you will start anew with the next day. This book is going to teach you that you will have to learn to leave those bad days behind. There is no benefit to those bad days except for what you learn from them. I will repeat that: There is no benefit to those bad days except for what you learn from them. You will learn that memories focused on bad days or bad things will only harm you. You must learn to forget about them. Happiness is not found behind you. It is found in front of you, quite literally, in both time and fact. Those things right in front of you that you choose to have around you, if chosen correctly, are going to give you an amazing life. It is the future time that allows you those experiences.

At the same time, you want to leave the negative behind you. You must learn to leave it far behind you so it is no longer thought of and a forgotten memory. I will repeat that one more time because of its importance. The negatives in life need to be left behind you so you can wholly focus on what's amazingly ahead of you. And notice I used the plural term, *negatives*, because they are just a fact of life. No matter how well you prepare, there will always be things outside your control that can be negative. My true hope is that you will learn to minimize and quickly get beyond all negative things that could make you lose focus on the great things that will also take place.

Before I leave this subject, let me give you an example scenario, or one of those fundamental analogies, to make my point. Let's say that you have been looking forward to a musical concert with excited anticipation. After all, this concert includes your favorite quartet that you have followed for years. You've even invited someone extra special to join you for the event, and you could not be more excited. But on the way to the event, you get pulled over by a policeman because your tag is unknowingly expired. You are only four blocks from the concert venue, and he knows you're going to the event and are excited to do so. But instead of writing you a warning, he writes you a very costly ticket. For a person who does not understand the critical elements, that ticket could ruin the concert.

I am going to teach a concept called compartmentalization later in this book. You have to learn to compartmentalize your thoughts. This means you get the negative thoughts out of your mind and focus on the future in a positive manner. You already know that you can address the ticket at a later date, and it has no relevance to the concert. Those are both facts. But if you keep thinking about that ticket or policeman, it will harm your experience at the concert. In this example, not only are you harming yourself, but also you are likely going to harm the experience of the person you are with because you're going to act differently. You have only four blocks to set aside this negative thought, and there is a clear motivation to do so. You want to maximize the joy of the concert with that special someone. You need to put that negative thought of the ticket so far behind you that it is not in your memory until a future date, when the ticket needs to be addressed. One objective system is to accept the ticket (because you don't have a choice), put a note on your calendar to address it on an appropriate date, and forget about it. It is as though you never received that ticket. Why? Because those negative things in life will only harm you. It is solely you who determines your happiness.

In this book, I am going to give you some tools for objective measures, which I call virtual compartments. There will be a compartment for good things. There will be compartment for not-good things. There will be a compartment for things you have to do. There will be a compartment for lessons you've learned. And because learning is a good thing, there will be a compartment for things you wish to learn. By starting off with these five compartments, you can easily recognize that you want the good things compartment to be a lot larger compared to the other compartments. In fact, you want the good things to be gigantic compared to the not-good things. The actual goal for you will be to totally forget about the not-good things compartment and thus empty it out, because there is no benefit for you to focus on negative things from the past. An important critical element for a happier life is to become an expert in compartmentalization.

This is not a book about the day someone hits the lottery, or the day the quarterback wins the big game. As mentioned earlier, the building block of time that I am using in this book is the twenty-four-hour period of a day. By looking at the length of time as a day, I also want to set standards for what happens in that day. In the past, you likely characterized days as a bad day or boring day or so-so day. My goal going forward is for you to be more focused on objective things that happen during the day. And when I say happen, I mean things that happen to you and things that happen because of you. In the end, I am going to help you to create amazing days—and a lot of them. The amazing day is not about an extraordinary day that can also happen but is less planned. I believe that everyone, young or old, rich or poor, weak or strong, can have a limitless number of amazing days. And the more amazing days you have, the more you'll look back and realize you're living a fabulous life. You will then also be excited about events that are in the future. It is critical that a great day today be followed up with as many amazing days in the future for a fabulous life. Don't aim low. Don't settle. Seek amazing in each and every day. The moment you think that all the great days are behind is the moment that you need to find new passions (plural). When I say don't settle, I encourage you to literally say out loud to yourself and those whom love you that you want more. If you have never spoken aloud to yourself, then you will experience a new feeling of happiness simply by saying out loud, "I want more." I hope I'm around to hear you say it, because it in turn makes me very happy. This is a book that will give everyone many objective and practical tools unique to the individual to increase the quality of your life by starting with the building block of amazing days.

To create an amazing day, you have to have the understanding or skill set to see what most would say are everyday events as being quite possibly extraordinary, and you have to learn how to create more of those events. As an example, most of us are quite accustomed to everyday activities such as walking. But in fact the ability to walk is actually an extraordinary collection of physiological factors that allow it to happen. Ask any biomedical engineer. In order to correctly walk, there is a staggering number of physiological things that must happen correctly. In simplistic terms, we have to have inner-ear balance, muscle control, and strength to maneuver. Yet most of us in good health take walking for granted. But suppose you got in a car accident and lost your ability to walk for a period of time. Now imagine that all of a sudden, after the accident, you get feeling back into your limbs, and you have the ability to walk again. What would that feeling be like? As you get deeper into this book, you'll begin to recognize that you alone are the one who controls your happiness, and there are many required facets to gain the greatest happiness. Here is another one of those especially important statements that I feel I need to repeat. You alone are the one who controls your happiness, and there are many required facets to gain the greatest happiness. One of those facets is to not take for granted as many things as you currently do. Do you take your marriage for granted? Do you take friendships for granted? Do you take your health for granted? Do you take your work for granted? Do you say "thank you" without truly meaning it? When was the last time you asked a loved one, "How can I make your day better today?" Or even better, when was the last time you focused your entire day on someone else? Have you ever taken the day off to arrange a great surprise for someone you love? That will be an extraordinary day not just for them but also for you. In fact, one of the things you're going to learn is that happiness is not all about you. You will learn that making other people, especially those who are part of your core of support, feel overwhelming happiness can make you feel extraordinary. You will learn that living your life for yourself, instead of with others, will not bring you happiness. The greatest life worth living is one where you focus on living it with others.

Here is an initial lesson: Stop taking things for granted. Start being more focused on life and thankful for things or people in it. Details matter, like paying your bills on time or sending out a thank-you to that person who did something kind for you or helped you out. Keys to having an amazing day include learning to recognize that amazing day and learning how to create one that is unique to you. Some amazing days are planned, and some just happen. This may sound counterintuitive, but you will see that amazing days will happen more often as you begin to create more planned ones. Without jumping too far ahead, you will learn that a fabulous life is not just about you. In fact, it is difficult to make absolute statements, but here goes one. You will be happiest in life when you share it. It is critical to happiness. I will repeat that critically important statement: You will be happiest in life when you share it. I'll give you a simple example. Let's say you struggled, quite literally, with attaining a college degree. Try to picture your graduation day. You're walking up the aisle and are about to step onto the stage. As you step toward the stage, you hear the family members cheering enthusiastically for the person in line in front of you as the president of the university reads her name aloud. The cheers are deafening. Now imagine yourself stepping onto the stage, and no one you care about is there to witness the event and share it with you. Who is experiencing the better graduation, although you're standing in the identical line and walking the exact same steps? As an absolute statement, I will state that happiness is not an asset that ever decreases by being shared.

There is a presumption in our society that wealthy or famous individuals have a lot of amazing days. There is an assumption that the wealthy or famous people will have more amazing days than those of us who are middle class or even less fortunate. The truth of the matter is that the amount of money you have in the bank does not determine happiness. Do you objectively think that a person who has ten thousand dollars in the bank is half as happy as the person who has twenty thousand dollars? Do you really think that if someone has over a million dollars in the bank, they are endlessly happy? There is objectively no direct relationship between wealth and happiness, and that is because life is so complex, there are many factors that go into creating true happiness. We'll be getting into those elements within this book. But let me repeat that there is no direct relationship between wealth and happiness—with just one exception. As I stated earlier, you cannot live beyond your means. You have to have your fiscal house in order. That said, even if money is a constant struggle for you, you still deserve an amazing day.

Can an amazing day just happen? Of course it can. In fact, it happens to many of those around us, but because of their attitude, they don't recognize it and let it slip by. One of the critical elements in life is to actually seek and look for amazing moments, and you will more likely create that amazing day. I will repeat that statement. One of the ways to make your life happier is to look for amazing moments in their many forms. Be thankful first thing in the morning, the moment you wake up. You can't have an amazing week, an amazing year, or an amazing life without the proper attitude. Also, be humble; the person who expects to be treated special will not appreciate as much as the humble person. The examples of amazing moments are as diverse as they are infinite, but you have to recognize them and focus on them even if momentarily. If possible, write the moments down. Again, you will learn that part of the critical elements is to put things in writing. Let me give you an example scenario as to why writing things down can literally change a so-so vacation into a vacation that can last forever, with the sole difference being taking a journal on the vacation. There is an objective and clear benefit to writing down the experiences you had at the end of each day of a vacation. First, you get to relive the day each evening. Who does not want to relive a fabulous day with vivid memories? Second, you have a lasting memory that you can refer to for years to come. Third, is that you will learn to be more focused on even the little things during a vacation. To understand the drastic difference, you merely have to objectively consider the differing scenarios. In one scenario, you go on vacation and record nothing. In a second scenario, you go on vacation and take some pictures. Notice that I said *some* pictures; I mean just a few to create the memory of the day. Too many folks make the mistake of missing a large part of their vacation experiences by taking too many pictures! There is a huge difference between walking through a stunning park and walking through a stunning park solely focused on taking picture after picture.

In a third scenario, you go on vacation, and at the end of each day, you and your fellow travelers sit around a table, perhaps during a great meal, and write down all the exciting things that happened during the day. Again, the memories are as diverse as they are infinite. Maybe you'll write down the cute laugh of the waitress or how fabulous the breakfast tasted. Neither of these can be captured on a camera. Maybe you write down the memory of watching a hot air balloon rise at night as the fire made it glow. Perhaps it was the cool breeze you felt during hiking, or the smell of the pasture. Perhaps it was the silly fall you took in the field when you accidentally tripped over a rock. And notice that I specifically used the word *memory* and the phrase *"end of the day."* Do not write things down as they happen. Never interrupt the experience itself. That is why taking pictures can ruin experiences when you take too many. You could be having the best day of your life, but you won't know it if you're always looking for something greener or better. Focus on fully enjoying the current day. You will have a totally different experience by continuously trying to take photos while walking along a gorgeous nature trail instead of simply walking along that same gorgeous nature trail but taking only one or two photos. Don't keep thinking about taking photos. Instead, focus on the people you're with or on nature itself. Photography is based on only what you see. What about what you hear, what you touch, what you are tasting and what you smell?

Part of the fun of the journal, which contributes to an amazing day, is to join together to repeat the experiences together from memory. I will also tell you that the most amazing moments may not be the stunning sunset or scene of a mountain snowcap. Don't get me wrong; they can also be amazing, but they are not the most amazing. The most amazing moment might be the moment your partner, out of the blue, stops on the trail, turns, looks into your eyes, and softly says, "I'd rather be here with you than any other place in the world. You still amaze me." As mentioned earlier, memories are more amazing when they are shared. That stunning sunset was pretty spectacular, but it is eclipsed by the moment you shared with your partner. Another benefit of these vacation journals is that you can reread them ten or twenty years later to create a fabulous evening. Maybe your children will read them someday so they can model their lives after yours.

Although I introduced these three scenarios as being on vacation, you should understand that this objective advice is not limited to vacations. You should understand that some of the most amazing moments in your life may in fact be when you find yourself at a specific place and at a specific time to help someone. Maybe it is with a smile. Maybe it is with a simple joke to make them laugh. Maybe it is to help someone with a car ride when it is raining or cold outside. Maybe it is anonymously leaving that big tip for the waitress working the night shift with taped glasses and an old car. When you are given that gift of being at the right place and at the right time, don't just consider helping—objectively act. You will never regret it. Then put it in your journal to reward yourself. Another rule is to ask yourself often if you've had an amazing day. I mean you should take a moment, stop thinking about anything else, and focus on that question and the answer to that question. Later in this book, I'm going to outline a specific, objective, yet simple system that you can practice, and I submit that you should make it part of your routine for the rest of your life. That simple system will help you capture and focus on those elements that create an amazing day. Remember and realize that what you can practice during a vacation scenario can be repeated in your everyday life. By the way, I am not presuming that everyone who reads this book will have the ability to take a vacation as that term is understood. But in fact everyone who reads this book can, and should, take mini vacations such as picnicking in a local park or walking the trails in a national park.

I think everyone should strive to have as many amazing days as possible. One of the critical elements is to also write down future goals to experience. Think of it as a bucket list. The goals could be simple. You promise yourself to go to a stage play at least once a year, or perhaps to start piano lessons. It might be to picnic at least once a month in the park. Perhaps it will be to go on one big vacation per year. Maybe it will be creating a special handshake with your best friend. Better yet, it could be learning the steps to a special dance with your daughter that someday you'll do with her on her wedding day. Without specific planning, without physically writing it down, the likelihood of you doing any of these things diminishes. I will repeat this statement: without specific planning, without physically writing down when you are going to do something, the likelihood of you doing it diminishes. The other benefit is that by writing the goal down, it becomes a more positive experience overall. If you suddenly go to Nashville last minute to catch a play, it is not as nice as planning to go to Nashville next month and choosing the perfect seat in the theater for a special play. By planning ahead, you get to look forward to actually going on the trip. You get to chat about it with others. You get to think about the clothes you'll be taking and the places you'll eat, and you can read about the folks in the play. I certainly don't mean to say that doing things spontaneously isn't exciting as well. Mixing up spur-of-the-moment activities and planned experiences is the best of both worlds.

As a note, please read this book slowly. I strongly suggest reading just one chapter a night and then pondering it for a day before you move onto the next chapter. Consider each sentence that I write. Also, I strongly suggest you keep this book as a reference. You will come to understand that your life's experiences will affect how you interpret this material.

Chapter Two

The Single Most Important Decision of Your Life: Who Will Be Your Lifelong Partner

NO MATTER YOUR INCOME, NO matter your level of education, and no matter your occupation, it is likely you will have at most only a handful of people in your life who are true advocates for you. And that is not a bad thing; that is simply the result of a busy life. We all grow up, and most of us go in different directions because of school, work, relationships, health, and more. What I mean by a true advocate is someone who truly wishes you a better life than them no matter how crazily happy they are. A person who wants you to laugh each and every day. A person who wants you to find love that others admire. A person who doesn't feel envy or jealousy toward you.

If we can think of a model for that person, most of us would think of an ideal parent, such as a mom or dad who loves unconditionally. When we look at relationships objectively, we should have models to compare them to so we know whom to truly trust. Can you trust every one of your siblings? Likely not, and that is okay. Families are not perfect. It is amazing how children raised in the same household can be so different.

You just happen to be born into that family. You had no choice in the matter, no input on the decision.

Let me get back to the topic of establishing a model that I touched upon earlier. A good way to envision a goal or objective is to recognize a model for achievement. For example, if you want to model what is a great home, you might look to a colonial or contemporary single-family home, depending on your tastes, with a two-car garage and a half-acre lot within walking distance to restaurants and shops. If you were to model a great performance of a team, you may look to a professional soccer team or American football team that put up some amazing statistics both offensively and defensively. If you want to model perfect love, you might want to think of the moment a mother first sees her newborn child. Notice that the perfect model for love is more time specific than a perfect home or perfect team performance. Also notice that a perfect team performance is not based on just a win. Let's say that a professional football team plays a mediocre college team and squeaks out a victory. Would anyone characterize that win as a model for a perfect performance of the team? No. And if I broadly say that perfect love is between a mother and her child, is that realistic? No. That same child at the age of fifteen can steal the car keys and speed down a road with an innocent passenger in the car. Would the mother feel the same "perfect love" when she learns what her child has done? Of course not. In the same regard, you cannot say that the model for a perfect love is a pet because that is a one-sided relationship based on need. If given a choice, are you certain that a pet would stay with its owner if it could leave the dog park with whomever it wants? The best type of love is one that exceeds the model of a mother being with her newborn for the very first time and repeating that moment for an unlimited period of time. Try to find a lifelong partner who can do that. One where passion does not end. One where longing does not end. One where a single lifetime is not enough.

Choosing your partner for life sounds almost ominous, and it can be. Yet few truly realize the implications or focus on the decision of choosing a lifelong partner. Many start a relationship on notions as shallow as "he/she is really cute." No one goes to the altar knowing the marriage is going to fail. In fact, they cannot be convinced of it. Yet factually, over fifty percent of marriages will fail. There are many marriages that are annulled because the marriage only lasts a few short weeks. Yet those same couples who seek the annulment could not be swayed from getting married just weeks earlier. I will repeat that over half of all marriages fail. Why does this happen? It's simple: Most couples never really know each other—or quite frankly, themselves. Many get married based on a pattern. If your parents married young, you'll marry young. If your "friends" are getting married, you'll have the desire to get married. I put the word "friends" in quotes because they are not really your friends as I think of the word. They are relationships or acquaintances but are not truly friends.

How many couples enter a marriage really believing or knowing what "to have and to hold from this day forward, for better, for worse, for richer, for poorer, in sickness and in health, to love and to cherish, till death us do part" truly means? You certainly cannot when you are high school sweethearts at sixteen. You don't even know yourself. You will most certainly change significantly from age eight to twelve. You will change from twelve to fourteen. You will change from fourteen to eighteen. You will change from eighteen to twenty-eight, and so on. What you thought was important in middle school or high school may seem like nonsense when you are in college. And what you thought was a priority in college, if you went to college, quickly changes when you get out in the real world and begin working. Consider the possibility that people change, and that includes you. You will not think ten years from now like you do today. In order to have the most rewarding and exciting lifelong relationship, you need to have a solid foundation based on knowledge gained from objective criteria.

What if your partner was in a car accident and lost both their legs below the knees just prior the marriage? Would you hesitate with the marriage? Would the thought enter your mind? Do you think that is the worst thing that can happen in a marriage? If you were truly passionate about the person you are about to marry, the auto accident would change nothing between you. After all, exactly what cannot be done with new lower legs? You can both still snow ski, run, go for walks, ride bikes, go to the movies, and dance. If you haven't found a lifelong partner, have you asked yourself why? Are you a partner someone would want for life? Is your priority finding someone with a large bank account? Are you closed off to anyone who doesn't have a college degree or graduate degree? I know these questions sound harsh, but please understand that I am being very objective with my questions in order for you to have an amazingly happy life.

Engineers model things. If you work on a team and say you want "a very efficient pump," engineers can get on the same page quickly by showing a sample of what is currently considered an efficient pump. Perhaps it dissipates heat quickly. Perhaps it has a minimum number of working parts. Perhaps it is highly efficient in pumping both fluid and vapor. The point is by modeling a pump, you can now objectively determine criteria that makes a pump very efficient as a team. It is vastly different from a homeowner hiring an interior designer and telling the interior designer to make her home beautiful. Well, what does that mean? Does that mean lots of plants? Does that mean bright colors? Does it mean trim details? If the homeowner is more specific by showing pictures, thus modeling what she thinks is beautiful, a quicker meeting of the minds can be reached. So how do you model love? And love is vastly different because it requires a two-way solution. After all, what good is a one-way love affair? The closest model to love is likely with a parent. But the type of love a parent provides is totally different than the love you seek from a lifelong partner. And a parent is not someone you choose. Does your parent love you less because you stole a car? What if you told your mom that your best friend's mom is a great cook and is really nice? Is your mom going to get jealous? Of course not. She's likely going to try to get your best friend's mom's recipe! Unlike simply being born into a family, that is the total opposite when it comes to choosing a life partner. The decision is wholly and solely yours.

A first objective, critical factor that is required of a life partner is your ability to fully trust them as you would your (model) parent. Choosing a life partner, who commonly becomes a spouse, is the most important decision you will ever make. As such, that life partner must be a person who is love and happiness combined. When you think of the term *love*, you think of that person first. And when I say *love*, I mean the "excited gut feeling when your partner walks into the room" type of love. The person who makes you look at the world with much more excitement because your partner has an interest in something you have never noticed before. It's the person who, when you see each other, you don't need to talk. You know so many times what each other is thinking without words. You can see it in their expression, which says, "Wow, you're still amazing," when they look at you. Yet you still feel a need to chat, even if briefly, for moments at a time so you can hear their voice, and you can instantly tell the emotion they are feeling. When you think of this person, it is a focused feeling that has you ignoring everything and everyone else in the room feeling. And when I say *happiness*, I mean the feeling of joy. If you were given the divine ability to be able to choose that one thing you couldn't lose, it would be that person. You would choose that person over losing nourishment, food, and even air so you could be certain that you'd die next to that person. That is a lifelong partner.

Happiness never decreases by being shared, and I can think of no greater level of happiness than sharing everything with your true life partner. It has been said that true love stories never have an ending. I certainly agree with that statement. I have met many older woman and men who have outlived their partners, and they still love to share stories of their courtships and fond memories with joy. It's a joy to hear the stories because their expressions and mannerisms also tell about the shared journey. I would say that true happiness is not a result of something that we receive but rather that we choose to share or give. You know that doing things with this person continues to feel amazing. A life partner is someone whom you want to make happier because it makes you feel fabulous to do so. You want that life partner to have a great day. And a true life partner feels the exact same way about you. It is someone whom you want to excitedly ask on a date when you're lying in bed at the end of the day after ten years of being together. That is an extremely high standard.

A second critical factor that a life partner must have is when you first meet this person, it is an immediate feeling of excitement. If someone asked me, "How do you know when you find that life partner?" I would answer it is when you find someone who is more beautiful on the inside than on the outside. Prepared to be amazed. There is no beauty without happiness. Happiness is a measure of inner beauty. Find someone who is happy by nature and witness the inner beauty that never diminishes. In the strongest of bonds, I have heard from both partners that they knew instantly. I objectively believe that you must actually feel that "love at first sight" type of excitement. I have spoken to many couples wherein the man tells me, "I saw her for the first time in a restaurant. We hadn't yet spoken. I already knew I was in love with her." I say "many couples" because this is not a rare occasion. I believe we all may have the ability to instinctively recognize someone who could be a lifelong partner if we are open to following our intuition or instincts. To be clear, there are huge differences between infatuation, lust, excitement, and deep-seated love. In the vast numbers of conversations I have had with couples both, or at least one of them, knew instantly that they had met someone amazing whom they wanted to learn more about. That theory held true for me. Trust your instincts to learn more about this person. You have that intuition for a reason. You may meet hundreds or even thousands of people in your career, but when you step into an elevator one day, you suddenly know you want to know more about that person who just captured your attention. Perhaps you are able to glance into each other's eyes for just the briefest of moments, and you saw that amazing smile. Or perhaps you're at a magic show, and suddenly your attention is drawn to the magician's assistant. Perhaps you're skiing down a hill, and you notice someone on the other side of the slope. Again, trust your instincts. There is a Five for Fighting song with the lyrics, "There's never a wish better than this when you only got a hundred years to live." When you find that incredible love, you wish that time would slow down because you only have a hundred years to live. You hear songs like "Wichita Lineman" by Glen Campbell and notice the lyrics "and I need you more than want you, and I want you for all time."

Alternatively, could there be a forever relationship where you have a mutual interest that grows for each other? Yes. But you have to also consider the fact that it could also mean that you are missing out on that *wow* factor relationship. Don't commit to a lifelong relationship based on "this can work," "it feels great," or "my friends really like them." This is solely your life decision. The odds are that if you are questioning the relationship to any degree, then it is not a forever relationship. Friends will come and go, so certainly don't base a relationship on what your "friends" think. Shoot for the highest standard of being amazed by your life partner. Given such a high standard for a life partner, it is objectively highly unlikely that a lifelong partner is a high school sweetheart or even a college sweetheart. That certainly does not mean you cannot meet your lifelong partner in high school or college. You might even meet your lifelong partner on the playground in elementary school. You never know when or where it's going to happen. But if you look objectively at those couples who marry young, the majority fail. That is objectively because you haven't even experienced life when in high school. You have no career. You have no idea what it's like to raise a child, much less a pet. But it is amazing how many high schoolers think they know everything. I was likely one of them. You don't know what you don't know—and what you don't know is a lot. This is also true for a college student. Yet it is not uncommon for a high schooler or college student to meet someone and honestly believe that the person is "the one." How does this happen? Simple: because you're not prepared.

Because this is such a sensitive subject, let me remind you of the objective of this book: your ultimate happiness in life. Thus when I make the statement that you are not prepared, I am being objective and not subjective. I was the same way; I also did not know it. How many relationships have you had such that you know this is the one? Do you realize that you are going to change in your life? For example, do you think that you are the same person now that you were when you were sixteen years old? How about when you were twenty-one? Did you think the same way in college as you did in high school? Do you really believe that you will think the same when you are out working as you did in college? Do you think you will think the same way once you experience life events like having a child? How about taking on the responsibilities of moving out on your own? How will the loss of a parent affect you? How about the loss of your left leg due to an automobile accident? Are you going to think the same if the cause of the accident is you instead of the other driver? If you are about to bring someone into your life at a young age, shouldn't you objectively understand that the person is also going to change? So what is the foundation that will keep you together forever? Do you both have identical core values? Objectively, you both are going to change. Remember that the standard for an amazing life is not just staying together. Did you have discussions with your parents or with your core of support before you met the new person? It is rare to ever hear of a parent who prepares their child for this relationship. These are the types of questions I consider before I make the statement that you are not prepared. This statement is not meant in a mean way whatsoever. Get that thought completely out of your mind. This analysis is not subjective; it is objective. My goal is for you to have the happiest life. A critical element to the happiest life is for you to share it with someone who amazes you for your entire life. And that other person must feel the exact same way about you as you both change. Has your partner ever told you that you amaze them? To get the full value of joy, you must have somebody to share it with. I want for you to start your future with the highest likelihood of meeting that high standard. Therefore, you should consider that I am correct if you are still in high school, or even college.

A third critical factor that a life partner must have is what I call a "list" factor that is unique to you. When you are seeking that amazing someone, you should have a list of the traits that you are looking for and have them written down. Do you even know how to begin a list of this magnitude? If not, you are certainly not ready for such a profound decision. That list should include questions that are important to you when selecting a lifelong partner. When you're wondering whether a person is special, you don't ask broad questions. Be more specific and ask questions that are most important to you. "Is this the man for me?" is too broad a question. Better questions are, "Does he make me feel secure? Does he make me laugh? Does he know the critical elements and actually use them?" What is your passion, and what are your needs? Do you have a passion for calligraphy, woodworking, volunteering at an animal shelter, traveling, home improvements, sports, politics, hiking, bowling, biking, ballet, opera, tennis, sewing, or perhaps an annual pilgrimage to Burning Man? Does this special someone have strong religious beliefs? What is his or her feelings on children? What if one of you can't have children? Where do you want to live? What type of housing do you hope to live in? What are all the costs on a monthly basis you expect to be paying as an adult? What percentage of our earnings do we need to save? What is their credit score, and what led to that score? Have you ever been arrested? Have you ever been drunk? Are you both going to work? What if one of you goes back to school? What if you lose your job? What are your political views? Who mows the lawn, and who paints? Who does the cooking? When bad things happen—and they will—do you see signs that your partner will fully support you, resulting in a closer relationship? Conversely, do you see signs that your partner tends to find someone to blame, and if it is you, it would result in pushing you apart? How exciting is the sex going to be? What are his friends like? Does he have friends, and if not, why not? Are their limits to what you wish to experience? Are your backgrounds similar? Was your partner given everything as a single child and thus expects a new car and maid service? Does your partner have a similar background as you wherein you understand that you have to work hard to both earn and maintain the things you own? Is your partner handy? Is your partner motivated? How long did their prior relationships last, and why did they fail? What are their best friends like? What are their parents like? Does this person respect both his parents? Does your partner like pets? A person who understands the critical elements will understand that they must objectively consider questions like these when making such an important decision. Does your partner treat others with kindness and respect? Is your partner able to laugh at their mistakes? Do you have similar senses of humor? Does your partner actually make you laugh? Is your partner a person with confidence? Do you both like to people watch? Have you ever been accused of flirting, thus perhaps pointing to a lack of trust or insecurity? Does your partner promise to never allow anyone to come between you? And "anyone" includes family including children. Are you your partner's highest priority, and is he/she your highest priority? When you meet with your partner's family, is there a change in your partner's character, or do you feel fully embraced?

It is common for folks to write a list when they go to the grocery store. I know folks who have written a list to purchase a car. If you start a business, you should have a business plan to create a clear objective for your business. When you build a home, you must have building plans. So if you are going to find this amazing partnership, shouldn't it objectively begin with a solid foundation of planning with written wants and needs? And shouldn't you be able to discuss each and every one of these questions together without hesitation? Building a business, building a house, buying a car, and going shopping are decisions that are minor compared to choosing a lifelong partner. If you've met a special someone, and that special someone doesn't have a list or doesn't immediately know the answers to your questions, then the odds of failure are high. That is because those who enter into those types of relationships don't know what they don't know.

This third list factor is critical to choosing a life partner, and you must be very honest in considering the list factors. You have to know that in most relationships the excitement of the initial relationship is going to recede. If you have found that amazing partner, then the initial excitement will not go away. As an example, even if you drive an amazing sports car every day, it is the first few drives that are the most exhilarating. The excitement is likely to mellow when the amazing sports car gets some wear and tear under the hood or breaks down. Therefore, you had better really love that sports car. You must realize that love cannot be based strictly on looks. With good health, you will both reach forty, then sixty, and then eighty years of age. It is the inner beauty that will still seduce each of you and excite each of you when you select your forever partner. Outer beauty is exciting at the beginning of a relationship, but it will never be the factor that creates a forever relationship. Do you love your mom and dad because of what they look like?

Let us get back to the critical list factors and honesty. Do not think that you found a forever partner if this special person fails in the critical list. Life is a very long time. Forever is an exceptionally long time. When you find that amazing person, you will think of them often, even after they have passed. If sailing is a passion of yours and thus on your list of questions in some form, and your partner can't swim and doesn't want to go on the boat, it's not a forever relationship. If you have a real interest in things mechanical, like bridge architecture, and this special person's only interest in mechanical things is the doorknob to the shoe store, then it is not forever. If you are budget conscious, and this special person doesn't know what saving means, then it is not forever. But on things that are more finite—you love horror movies, but this special person abhors them—then you will be surprised at how the *wow* factor will have you give up those movies because it forces time apart. I am also not saying that individual interests in a relationship are not a great thing; in fact, it can function as a strong bond between you if you both enjoy private time. Trust your instincts when you find a person to learn more about them. But just because your instincts tell you that this person is someone you need to learn more about you have to be honest with the third critical element list. Perhaps you were drawn to this person because of their outer beauty. I will state with absolute clarity that outer beauty is nothing compared to inner beauty. It is the inner beauty that brings forever happiness. There is no "one fits all" model except for the fact that all of these first three critical elements should be objectively recognized if you hope to find that person that you can't be without.

Do not be afraid to end a relationship when you are honest about the list factors. I fully understand that no one likes to end a relationship. But again, forever is a long time, and you don't want to settle for just a good life. You should strive for an amazing life. To have an amazing life, you need an amazing partner. Don't settle, because when you find that special person you will be amazed. Focus on an amazing life in front of you. There is no benefit to looking back at any failed relationships. By looking backward, you may fail to see an amazing person right in front of you. That amazing someone is out there for you.

Notice that when I introduced the third list factor, I stated *when* you are seeking. *When* refers to a time in your life when you're ready to think of finding that lifelong partner. And exactly when you should think of finding that lifelong partner is when you're ready and not before. This is an objective and very personal decision. It is hopefully a lifelong decision you are going to make. You should understand its profound importance. Are you ready to make such a profound decision before you even graduate high school? Before you graduate college? Before you begin your career? Do you even know what you want at this point in your life, even before you move out of your parents' home or before you own your first car? Does your potential partner fully understand what they want in life? All these decisions are minor compared to choosing a lifelong partner. Why? Because you don't know what you don't know. If you don't know enough to purchase a home, I would objectively submit that you don't know enough to make a far greater decision.

A fourth critical factor in deciding on a life partner is that once you meet the person who feels incredibly special to you, do not be in a hurry. You are talking about your whole life and the happiness a fabulous partner will bring to it. Allow a great amount of time and experiences to happen before you make a greater commitment. When you first meet someone, your attraction can be referred to as the honeymoon period. Everything will seem exciting. But you can only kiss that person for the first time once. You can only caress that person for the first time once. It is a time when lustfulness will be a factor. What is the relationship going to be like one thousand kisses from now? What will it be like after doing the laundry for a full year? What will it be like after cleaning dishes for two years? Again, it is rare to meet a person who actually has a list of priorities for a life partner. At the time of writing of this book, I have never met one. But the list factor is a critical element. I had a list because this is the most important decision I was ever going to make. And if you actually write down a list, it makes decision making totally different than merely thinking about general traits. Let me also repeat that you must not be in a hurry to advance your relationship to a greater commitment. The reason I state you must let a great amount of time and experience to happen is because you need to understand the true character of a person. You should understand that the more you commit to a relationship, the more difficult it is to end when it is not the forever relationship. It will be more difficult to be honest with the person you're with, and with yourself, when suddenly you meet that amazing person.

You should also understand objectively that the more money you make, the more attractive you look in our society. That is simply a fact. If you question my objective statement, just ask yourself questions of fact. If a guy arrives in a Ferrari to an event versus arriving in a Kia, who is going to get greater attention at the event? Is the beautiful supermodel going to look at the incredibly nice, funny, sincere, and hardworking manager at the grocery store, or is she going to be more interested in the famous sports player? I submit this also holds true for any financially successful person. The higher your position, the more likely to gain the attention of those who wish to form a relationship with you. You need to be objectively aware of this fact. One of the reasons that relationships fail is because of financial pressure and expectations. To avoid these false relationships based on financial success, I submit once again that you must give a great amount of time and experiences, in combination with the other critical factors, before you advance any commitment in a relationship. What is the hurry? If someone genuinely loves you, then time is not going to change anything except to reinforce your relationship. In fact an objective measure in a forever relationship is that it is always getting better and better. If not, you are not in a forever relationship.

When asking about a fabulous relationship, the question shouldn't be, "What is your secret for being married for fifty years?" Why is there an assumption that if a couple is together for fifty years, it was a fantastic marriage? Why would time be the litmus test for happiness? If you went on a date for the first time with a man who is thirty-five years old, and he told you he still lives with his parents, would you immediately think, "Wow, you must live in a very happy household"? Of course not. Just because you've continued in a living situation for many years doesn't mean that it must be a great living situation. People stay in marriages for all kinds of reasons. A person who understands the critical elements not only will have a better marriage but also will have a marriage that continues to grow in intensity and excitement. A couple that understands the critical elements is able to have fully open communication, which is a key element within a fantastic marriage. If you don't know the critical elements, then you don't know what you don't know. If you don't understand something, how would you know to ask the right questions?

When I meet couples that appear incredibly happy together, my first thought is not to ask them how long they have been together. Instead I ask them, "Could your life have been more wonderful?" I would not be surprised if they both looked at each other, laughed, and without hesitation answered, "Absolutely not." The laughter is interesting because it means that they likely had some private moments that immediately came to their minds in a similar manner that made them laugh. The immediacy of the answer means they didn't have to think about what-ifs. That means their happiness was not based on whether they had more money or whether they had met someone else. They both realize that their sharing of life was a critical element to not only their happiness but also their partner's happiness. One of my follow-up questions might be directed to the wife: "Would you still like to go on a date with your husband tomorrow?" I ask that question because the happiest marriages are not assumed. People who love each other don't take each other for granted. They continue to want to please the other. It is very selfless. The best marriages are when both in the marriage continue to date each other. One may bring home a gift just because they saw something they knew the other would love. One may write a handwritten letter to the other and put it in the mail. It is "just" a hand-written letter that talks about meeting this special person at breakfast this morning and missing that special person by the time lunch rolled around. The letter recounts how they couldn't make it past early afternoon before they needed to hear the other's voice. And when they got home, their partner was more beautiful than on the day they first met. That is just a simple letter to some, but not to a couple with a fabulous marriage and an amazing partnership. That is a type of relationship that is most rewarding in life.

In a relationship where they still date each other, there is no quid pro quo. Just because the husband gives his wife a foot massage, that doesn't mean she must give him a back massage. The husband simply knows that his wife loves a great foot massage, and he is hoping to get another date the next day. Okay, maybe a date plus benefits. Has your husband suddenly stopped in the middle of mowing the lawn and then found you in the garden just to tell you he misses you and that you're amazing? Has your wife stopped in the middle of doing dishes, wrapped her arms around you, and kissed you without having to say a word? That is a fabulous marriage. Thus a factor in finding that forever relationship is that you factually can't know if it's going to be a fabulous relationship without time and experiences. It is terrible to objectively consider that people can act in a certain manner just to get something they want. People can be fake, especially during dating, and trust can be earned only with time. How thankful are you for your partner or what are the signs they are thankful for you? Exactly how do you show your partner that you are thankful? Have you written your partner a letter lately? Have you purchased your partner a card? Have you made dinner reservations at a special restaurant without a special occasion? Have you made a special meal at home? Do those tasks take too much effort? If they do, what does it mean about your thankfulness?

What if you're reading this book, and you objectively realize that you're not in that *wow* relationship? Can you make it one? Absolutely. But it takes two. And you have to objectively consider that you are part of the reason that you are not in a relationship that everyone else admires and talks about. You are not in a relationship where a stranger walks up to you and says, "You two look incredibly happy together." Objectively speaking, if you are not part of the reason that you are not in a *wow* relationship, that means your partner is totally to blame. Do you think a discussion with your partner, telling them that they are the reason you are not in an exciting relationship, so it is totally their fault, is a good way to start a conversation? I would suggest the best way to get back to an exciting relationship is to start dating each other again. Begin by learning about each by starting fresh and focusing on listening. After all you are now different people with more life experiences. Go on a first date… again. I also realize that if you are not yet in a relationship, this chapter of the book is going to be of great interest to you. It is giving you knowledge about relationships. But a reader who is already in a relationship is likely going to be defensive. Because I am raising this issue, it is clear that I understand the human factors. No one wants to admit they might have made a bad decision, especially when it comes to sharing your entire life. Here is a simple measure to consider to determine whether you're in a great relationship. If someone was watching you interact with your partner twenty-four hours a day, would that person say you two look incredibly excited to be together? Would that person say you two look very much in love?

If you are already in a relationship, do not take your marriage for granted. When you take things for granted, you objectively tend to appreciate it less. You take it for granted that your car will start. You take it for granted that you will not be fired from your job. You take it for granted that your husband will be home for dinner. You should objectively realize that whatever you take for granted, that means you don't appreciate it as much. This lack of appreciation will affect your partner and your relationship. Do not assume your partner still finds you exciting or sexy. That does not mean that your partner does not find you exciting or sexy. I am simply saying you should not assume it. Assume the opposite and see how exciting things can become in your relationship. If you were trying to seduce your partner for the rest of their life, what would be your next step? After that first step, the next step is going to start with communication. And here is the fun part: it can be very intimate communication. Is there a secret or two, of the intimate nature, that you want to discuss? When was the last time you told your partner about what still amazes you about your partner? Tell your partner about any dreams you may have or goals you'd like to reach. Make sure you listen to theirs, and then help each other to make as many of those dreams come true as possible. One way to keep a relationship exciting is to literally ask if they find you exciting or sexy. Alternatively you can literally ask them how you can be more exciting or sexy. Ask the question and then just listen and don't hurry the answer. You might both dream of a trip to Spain, but perhaps that money went to a new refrigerator, so you promise a sexy dinner to each other at your favorite Spanish restaurant, followed by a Spanish love story movie where you read all the subtitles in a candlelit living room. If you are not yet in that lifelong relationship, the important thing to realize is that you must have all four critical factors to have an amazing life partner. A failure in any of the four factors means that you should not commit to a lifelong relationship with this person. If you understand the four critical factors you will know why that statement is true. But when you meet that person who does meet all four critical factors, be prepared to have an amazingly happy life while you have each other. Be the envy of the neighbors and your family members.

By the way, if you've been married for ten years without your husband stopping the lawnmower, you can maybe change that. You can add excitement to your relationship by stopping him the next time he mows the lawn. Remember, you have to be objective and consider the possibility that it is you who has not added excitement to the relationship or it is you that has taken the relationship for granted. What is an objective standard of knowing if you have a great relationship? You may think that you have a great relationship because you don't know what you don't know. But you are only half of a relationship. So the real question is, Do you both genuinely believe you have a great relationship? If you do, then that is all that matters. Talking about why you still love each other on a regular basis cannot be understated, but if you want an objective measure, there are some simple ones. Perhaps one could say that you have a fabulous partnership if you could say, "I already miss my partner when I back out of the driveway, even though we've been together for fifteen years." Do you both have a need to reach out to each other multiple times a day? Do you both feel that you need to touch when you're walking side by side? Do you communicate with a look or gesture? Do you have friends telling you that you two have a great relationship or that you look incredibly happy together? Do your friends comment that they see you laughing a lot together? Do they mention that they notice how you're always touching each other or glancing at each other? Do they mention that they wish they had a relationship like yours? Comments like these are an outsider's view of your happiness, and that is something you should be proud of. Because not only are you likely very happy in your relationship, but you're also teaching others (like your family and friends) what their relationship could be. It is the perfect opportunity to share with them why your relationship is amazing. Those comments from others are also a good way to keep your relationship very caring. You could ask yourself, "What would someone say if they saw us acting this way toward each other?" Couples that are constantly dating (by not taking their relationship for granted) show their compassion, their thankfulness, their desire, their respect, and their admiration for each other, and they are happier.

I remember being in a crowded outdoor park when I saw two younger people waving at each other. The man walked hurriedly to the woman, and they quickly embraced. I noticed they were married by the rings on their fingers. I don't know how long they had been married because I never approached them. I simply felt joy in seeing their happiness. But I also thought to myself how happy I am that after many years of marriage, I still feel that same excitement with my wife. In fact, it has grown stronger, yet I could not believe that was possible when I first met my wife. To this day, I still want to rush to her, and I hope someone is watching us like I watched those two young people, to see how amazing a forever love can truly be.

When thinking of a life partner, consider creating that list, but it has to be a very honest list. The critical elements are very objective and logical. Thus, someone with an understanding of the critical elements would rank items on the list. Perhaps they are called virtues or personal traits. I will tell you at the top of that list are kindness, honesty, and intelligence. In our society, you must objectively realize that youth, beauty, and perceived wealth are seductive, and thus someone with all three is perceived to be a real catch, especially if it is sexual beauty. A partner is most seductive when we are young ourselves and seduced by others' youthful and beautiful appearance. Thus if youth and beauty are on the top of your list, you had better have a prenuptial agreement ready, because you'll be using it shortly; there is a remarkably high probability that that relationship will fail. A person with the understanding of the critical elements realizes that inner beauty is much more important than outer beauty. Let me repeat that: Inner beauty is much more important than outer beauty. Now, don't get me wrong. Outer beauty is important in general terms because you need to be attracted to your partner. But you must realize the fact that outer beauty is not forever. True inner beauty is forever. That is what kindness is, and it is the most seductive thing you'll ever witness or experience once you find someone who truly possesses it. It's the person who, innately and without recognition, holds the door for that other person. Who helps the mom in the parking lot load the heavy items into her car. Who shovels the sidewalk in front of the neighbor's house. It's the woman who, at the register, sees a family putting things back because they can't afford them, and she quietly tells them it would be her pleasure to make the purchase for them. It's the delivery woman who holds the hand of the elderly person on the porch and chats for a period of time even though she has to complete all her deliveries and is already running late. It's the military man in heavy traffic who changes the tire on a stranger's car when he is running late for a meeting. Or perhaps it's the woman who answers the Christmas wish when she finds a card to Santa by chance. Those are the people who love naturally. Find them. That's where you should start.

As I have gotten older, I have also wrestled with a belief, a possibility, that each of us was actually made for someone. Remember that I am a man of science. I look at facts and am very objective. But if this belief is true, it would further prove the importance of the second critical element. After all, if you had the ability to give the greatest gift in the world, what would it be? Would it be money? Would it be material things? Would it be forever life? I could think of no greater gift than giving someone the perfect companion. That someone would be an amazing reward each and every day of your life. That someone, that person, makes every day of your life better. Perhaps all of us are given a path that will lead us to that person just briefly. What would happen if you could find that person somewhere in the world? Would you instinctively feel it? I believe you feel something immediately when you meet that potential someone. I don't know if "someone" means only one. But I know the instinct is true because it happened to me. When you meet that partner, you feel something totally different. There is a complete wow factor. And if that path leads to a such an amazing person, it will also logically mean that whoever established that path wanted us to be good all along that path. While on this path in life, we are all given free will. If you choose to get off that path of doing good, you will lose not only the ultimate reward of finding that someone but also the other rewards along the way.

Making a bad decision is not just a one-off with a small effect. Using free will to be mean to others, to be envious, to be egotistical, to seek drugs, to stay with false friends, to harm your body with excessive alcohol or drug abuse, or to overeat all have other ramifications. One of those ramifications is to knock yourself off your path of happiness at any time. I have learned that in life, there is no such thing as a one-off. If you are a person of character, you are not going to steal an unlocked bike. You are not going to need to see what it feels like to be drunk. And if you are going to do those wrongful things, I believe you are off the path that will bring you the ultimate in happiness. You were not created to steal. You were not created to harm someone else or yourself. You were not created to be lazy. All of these actions have numerous consequences that you cannot see, and you will never know because you choose to take the wrong path in life.

I can objectively give you an example of what I mean when I say one action is not isolated, a one-off, but is actually connected to other outcomes in your life. You simply don't know it. Find and ask a person who you believe may have lost a tremendous amount of weight. It's a simple objective question to ask someone. Did you lose a significant amount of weight? If that person answers yes, you should ask a follow-up question: Was another part of their life affected? After all, "all the person did" was lose some weight. You will find that that one "simple," positive change in their life has had a ripple effect that they were not aware of before the weight loss. They perhaps have more confidence. They have more energy. They sleep better. The reverse is logically true when you make the "simple" change of getting drunk. Perhaps you chose to get drunk because you thought something was missing in your life, and you thought it would be cool to try something new. Perhaps you are letting others make decisions for your life and are following your peers. For whatever reason, you have veered from your path to the happiest life. And although you may think getting drunk at that party was really cool, what you don't know is that your lifelong partner was at that same party, and you never met because of your one-off decision. Or perhaps if you hadn't gone to the party, you would have met your lifelong partner at the golf tournament you were going to attend instead. The simple fact is that you will never know.

If you have any doubts—and I mean *any* doubts—do not go forward with marriage. There is no hurry in getting married. Be absolutely honest with your partner about those doubts. After all, if you are going to have a lifelong commitment to someone, there can be absolutely no secrets. Everything is on the table to discuss, and I mean everything. Find someone who feels you're the most important person in the world and in their life. Find a person who asks, How can I make your life better? How can I do more?" Find someone amazing. Find someone who is never impatient, is never condescending, focuses on you, and is confident. Forget politically correct rules. Behind closed doors, in private, be open and honest. Your partner must love you just as much as you love them. And when it comes to your core principles, your lifelong partner has to have most if not all of those same core principles. What are your priorities, and what are your partner's? You and your partner must write them down individually before you reveal them to each other. Write those core principles down before you discuss them, otherwise your partner will simply agree with you to keep you happy. Your conversations should never be one-sided. For example, if you're discussing your core principles, you should take turns stating what is a core principle. That is a totally different conversation than you listing five core principles and your partner saying they agree with all five and ending the conversation. You must be honest and know what you need in a forever partner, not just what you want. Have a higher standard. I will repeat that: You must be honest and know what you need in a forever partner, not just what you want. Find the kindest heart, even if that person is a professional wrestler. The inside can be totally different than the outside. A beautiful woman who doesn't realize she is beautiful is incredibly beautiful on the inside. Find inner beauty and natural kindness.

A final thought before I leave this chapter. If you are an adult reading this for the first time, note that you can prepare a preteen or teenager with this information. Education prior to any experience is always better than trying to find an answer during an experience. As an example, learning what to do before you drive on ice is more preferable then trying to figure out how to drive on ice once you're on it. A person educated about driving on ice may be prepared with chains, studded tires, bags of sand, and survival gear in the trunk. Those without education about driving on ice will finds themselves greatly unprepared compared to those who have been prepared.

Chapter Three
What Friends Really Mean

A CRITICAL ELEMENT TO A happy life is to choose to be around those who inspire you. The role of positive friendships is critical because a solitary life without friends is not a happy life. This is especially true prior to you finding a forever partner. True friends will understand that should you find that amazing forever partner, and when you fall in love, hanging with your best buds isn't as much a priority. Notice that I stated *positive* friendships. Simply having friends is not enough for the happiest life. You need positive friends. Exactly what does a positive friendship mean? It means a friendship that is making your life better. You may have friends from work, from earlier in your life, from your school, from your neighborhood, from a bowling league you joined, or from doing volunteer work. Maybe it is a sibling or other family member. However you met these friends, you need to ask yourself some very important questions. Are these friends encouraging you in a positive manner? Are they making your life better by encouraging you to do things that will benefit you in life? Are they supporting you in getting a higher degree or going back to school to learn a new trade? Are they encouraging you to follow your dream of being an entrepreneur? Are they helping you manage your time or helping you do that volunteer work? Are they encouraging you to stick to that exercise routine? Can you call them up to help you clean out the garage and be confident they will show and be ready to work? Are they good listeners who are helping to inspire you, versus discouraging you from reaching your potential and goals?

For a good person, it is difficult to be angry for an extended period of time. It is actually exhausting and stressful. You will find that striving for love and kindness is a much easier path than seeking hate or anger. You will find that extreme happiness gives you almost boundless energy. The same can be said for those who are around you. It is stressful if you surround yourself with angry people, depressed people, envious people, arrogant people, or people who think they are superior to others. Conversely, if you surround yourself with positive people, you'll feel better about yourself. Positive people not only objectively reduce stress but also energize and motivate others. The best of friends are those who positively reinforce you to reach your goals and dreams. This is not the same as someone who asks you to join them for lunch and then tells you all the bad things in their life. Is this so-called friend someone who also tells you the path is too hard and the hurdles are too high? Is this friend someone who blames others for not reaching their own goals? It's easy to blame others. Blame old people. Blame short people. Blame the weather. Blame the hot sauce. What is the benefit of that blame? You need to look forward. Blaming others is never a solution; it is simply a negative crutch to reinforce failure.

Why must you ask these very important questions? Because objectively, you will become like those with whom you associate. I will repeat that: you will become like those with whom you associate. If you associate with a group of military folks, you will learn concepts like honor, integrity, trust, and teamwork, and you will truly understand what they mean. If you associate with folks in the medical field, you will learn compassion and assistance. And if you associate with folks who feel strong about their faith, you learn prayer and forgiveness. But if you associate with a group of thugs, you will learn concepts like stealing and hateful acts toward others. If you associate with people who get tattoos, you will have discussions about tattoos and likely get one too. If you associate with friends who give you reasons why you will not reach your goals, then the likelihood is you will not reach them. Those folks are not friends. Do yourself a favor and find yourself some new friends. You may not realize it, but they are limiting your growth and your potential. Most certainly they are limiting your happiness. I also fully understand that it is not enjoyable to end friendships, but you can do so subtly so as to not hurt other's feelings. You don't need to say, "I don't want to be your friend anymore." You can simply be too busy if they reach out to you on multiple occasions. You can create an excuse of not feeling up to doing something. You can also choose to be honest with them and tell them why you need to end the friendship. I don't want this to sound harsh, but your happiness is more important than the feelings of a negative friend.

Do you hang around with folks who try to do their best, or do you hang with a group that seems to be always searching for something to do? Do you hang around a group of angry people? If so, you will find that you will become angry. Do you hang around a group that is envious of others? Then you will become envious of others. Do you ever take time to consider the influence your friends are having on you? Did you suddenly think about getting a tattoo because your friends got tattoos? Did you get your ears pierced four times because you think four piercings make you more beautiful than just one or two piercings, or were you influenced by others? Did you look in the mirror and consider all the different types of earrings instead of getting yet another piercing? Are you feeling a desire to get married because all your friends are getting married? Are you feeling a desire to have a child because you have siblings who are having children? If your friends are buying a house, do you now feel a desire to buy a house? Is that the happiest way to live your life? No. If you want to look at what you'll become in three years or less, look at your friends. I will repeat that: If you want to see what you'll become in three years or less, then look at your friends. If your friends gossip, do you think they do not gossip about you? If your friends are unfaithful in their relationships, do you truly think their relationship with you is steadfast? If your friends are critical of other people, do you really think they are not critical of you? And if you hang around folks who gossip or are critical of others, you will find that you will become that way. If your friends play golf, you will likely take up the game. If your friends have a cocktail at the end of a round of golf, you will begin to have a cocktail too. If your friends drink a specific vodka, you will begin drinking that vodka. How many things do you do because of the influence of others? Where do you shop, what do you wear, whom do you vote for, what type of vehicle do you drive, and what music do you listen to? The list is almost endless.

I will give you an objective yet simple example of what I mean. I have a daughter who started high school, and I noticed within about four weeks that she started to include the word "like" in her speech. It was a trait she had never had before. Yet within just a very short time, with a new group of acquaintances in school, she took on their speech habits. It got progressively worse. Almost every sentence had the word "like" in it. Her injection of "like" into her speech got so bad that I had to take steps to correct it. She had not noticed how bad it had gotten herself. This was a trait that she unknowingly gained from those she associated with. As a side note, my solution to this speech problem was solved using a fun family game. As we gathered for dinner, I would select a topic, completely unknown to her, and she had to talk about the subject for a timed full minute without using the term "like." For example, perhaps the topic was "a summertime game", "how to ride a bike", or "whom do you admire and why". If she could not speak on the topic for a full minute, I would select a new topic and start over. She soon was able to beat the habit, and perhaps more important, she heard the improper speech pattern in her group of school friends and others. I was also able to use this as a lesson for her to understand: "You will become like those you associate with". If these school friends are teaching bad speech, what else are they teaching her that she may not even be aware of?

Find friends who inspire you. Find those that challenge you to be more polite, more knowledgeable, more loving, more respectful, and more humble even though you know that you are valuable. Find those that keep you excited about a sport or activity. Get away from those who teach you to be more sarcastic, more egotistical, more derogatory, or more ridiculing. Find friends who have a great amount of knowledge in your field of interest so you can improve your knowledge in your field. Find friends who find joy in life and follow in their path. Find friends who have great relationships with their parents and then copy what they do and improve upon it. Do not simply select friends because they have a similar passion to yours or work in your same building. For example, perhaps you love surfing. All your friends should not be surfers, unless those surfers are all of positive character. They will certainly be acquaintances because you tend to surf at the same time and in the same location on certain days of the week. But a true friend has to be much more than one who shares a common interest or passion. They must be of positive character. A friend is a person with whom you share a strong bond. An acquaintance is someone who is known but who is not a close friend. Yet most of us use the term *friend* and never use the word *acquaintance*, as though having more *friends* is important or makes you feel better. It is quite the opposite. If you die with five friends around you, then you likely had a fulfilling life. If you go to a crowded funeral wherein the person is not famous and is not associated with a large business, then that person was likely amazing in life. Strive to be amazing. Be a person whom others care for because you cared for them. A person who has a huge number of friends is likely not a friend to anyone. For example, if you moved, if you changed jobs, or if you needed money, how many of those friends would call you just to chat with you on the phone? Yes, actually hearing someone's voice or getting a written letter is factually different than simply staying in contact on social media. A true friend calls and sends a letter on special occasions, or just because they are thinking of you. Those who are true friends are not those found only through social media. Picture the person you care for most in your life right now. Would you consider not talking to that person for the next five years and only using social media, email, or text to communicate? Would that be fulfilling? Objectively, that proves that those who communicate only in that manner are not your true friends, and you are wasting your time checking social media more than just a limited amount of time. The time you are spending with social media is time you are not experiencing a more rewarding life. During that same time period you could be volunteering, learning how to speak a foreign language, actually talking to your true friends and loved ones, or doing a plethora of other things.

Follow your instincts when it comes to friendships. Are people in your core of support telling you to end a relationship or get away from a certain group or person? Quite often you are aware that you should be moving on, but you fail to end the friendship. You did not want to upset your friend. You are kind by nature and don't like ending relationships. As a side note, being naturally kind is not a weakness. In fact, I find it a gift to meet people who are naturally kind. Do not confuse kindness with mental or physical weakness. Some of the most beautiful people are both mentally and physically strong yet incredibly kind. Unfortunately, it is the person who is most kind who is most easily taken advantage of in terms of a relationship. It is the kind person who will lend money, let you borrow a car, watch a pet, or go to a party to support a friend. If you are one of these kind people, you have to understand that these false friendships are holding you back from true happiness. These negative friendships are preventing you from reaching your potential and finding positive friends. If you are not willing to end those negative relationships, then you are not willing to start new ones to your own detriment. Your tomorrows will be just like yesterday because you're not willing to change your relationships. What is your vision for tomorrow? You have a very happy and meaningful life to lead, but not if you attach yourself to the wrong friends. Those negative friends are taking you from the path of your greatest happiness. They can and will negatively affect your work, your passions, and even possibly your lifelong relationships. Do not listen to a person who tells you that you'll always struggle or won't advance.

I mentioned earlier that even siblings or family members might not be the best of friends. Do you have family members who tell you that college is out of reach for you? Do they tell you that because you are not part of a wealthy family, you are at a disadvantage? A family member, or any friend, who is teaching you a defeated mindset is stunting your growth. Do they tell you that no one in your family has ever gone to college? Do they explain that none of your parents, grandparents, or great grandparents went to college? Do they blame others for circumstances? Do they tell you that things will never work out for you? A person who tells you these things is not a friend, and more than that, they are limiting your true potential. That is not someone who inspires you. Do not let someone talk you out of your dreams. That is not someone who is encouraging you to reach your goals. That is not someone helping you to find a solution to a problem you may face. That is not someone who is helping you to reach your true potential. Does that same family member tell you that opening up your own business is too risky? Do they tell you about their own negative experiences? Do yourself a favor. Find yourself some new friends who aspire to go to college or graduate school, or medical school, or vocation school. Ask how they are doing it. Define a first step and achieve it. Then take the next step and so on. Find some friends who have started a business and ask them how they did it. There will be failures—what I call rough pebbles—along your path but they are not roadblocks. Everyone in life experiences good friendships as well as betrayals. We all experience ups as well as downs, victories as well as losses, promotions as well as setbacks. Do not allow fear of future betrayals, setbacks, or losses affect your character or determination, except to make you stronger. They are merely detours that you can learn from.

Also, do not believe the media claims that we all live in dysfunctional families. That does not have to be true in your life. You are solely responsible for the decisions you make. Set a higher standard for your life. Become the model for other family members. Show them that you all can succeed. You can break that chain and buy a home. You can achieve that high level of education. You can get out of debt. You can stop that addictive behavior. Stop accepting the lie that things are not going to work out for you. You are harming yourself more by not starting something because of a fear of failure than by trying and failing. You will learn that failure is a lesson and a starting point for something new and better. How high can you go if there is no such thing as fear?

If your friends have a defeatist attitude, then how are you going to achieve your potential in life? I'll give you a real-world example. Imagine having a coach who gives a speech before a big game that it is okay to lose. A coach that tells his team that it was a fluke for them to even be at the tournament. A coach that tells his team that they really didn't earn the right to play in the game. Imagine a coach who tells his team that the school district has never made it to the state finals, and thus there is no expectation to win. What are the odds that a team given such a speech could win? Now, take the exact same team wherein the coach tells them that each of them is about to achieve greatness, and as a team, nothing is out of their reach. What are the odds that the team may go on to win? And that was just one speech. What are you hearing every day from your friends? Do you even recognize the fact that you're repeating the word "like" in every sentence? My hope is that you can see that you can achieve greatness in the game, despite the coach's terrible speech. You can cause the interception. You can score the goal. You can sprint to the finish ahead of everyone else. My hope is that you will also consider trying to convince others to do the same and try their hardest. And I hope that you are now wise enough to seek a new coach and perhaps an entirely new team. If you have great character and integrity and give it your all, then you've accomplished it all. You gave it your best. After all, that is the most you can ask, and it will give you the greatest joy in all aspects of your life.

If you have a poor self-image or low self-esteem, perhaps these were learned from others. Are you afraid to step out and take the lead? Do you feel insecure? Were those traits learned? You must consider the fact that it is likely others that have caused you to have those thoughts. What if instead, you believed that you were meant to lead this project at work? What if instead, you believed you could make that team with hard work? What if you knew you could solve that problem? What if you knew you could reach that goal? Stop believing lies that you are never going to succeed. No one knows the future, and you can begin on a new path today. Consider the possibility you don't feel that level of confidence because you have not learned it as a skill, and possibly you have been taught the opposite without realizing it. I was never taught confidence. What if you had friends who wanted to become professional athletes, or medical doctors, or masters in chess? Do you think a professional athlete who takes the field for the first time is certain he will make all the proper plays? No, he is going to improve with time, but he has the confidence to start that learning process. Do you think a doctor who performs surgery for the very first time has the same level of confidence as a physician who has performed the same surgery one thousand times? No, but she is also going to improve her skill set over time. Do you think the chess player who enters his first tournament is confident he will make every proper move? It is very unlikely that someone can be that brilliant, and he will learn by his mistakes. If you understand that everyone is likely to fail to some degree when they try something new, you should recognize the same about yourself. The key to success is starting. That is how you gain confidence and knowledge. And you will learn as an adult that many elements of happiness are tied to knowledge and experiences. I will repeat that because of its importance. Happiness is directly tied to positive experiences. I stated *"as an adult"* because the innocence of a child finds happiness in almost anything. As we become adults and begin to understand the needs of self-reliance, the innocence of childhood sadly goes away.

Let me give you one more example to illustrate the objective difference of what positive friendships can mean within the setting of your health. According to the Mayo Clinic's website, "Friends also play a significant role in promoting your overall health. Adults with strong social support have a reduced risk of many significant health problems, including depression, high blood pressure and an unhealthy body mass index (BMI). Studies have even found that older adults with a rich social life are likely to live longer than their peers with fewer connections." That does not mean that having more friends is better. Mayo Clinic's website also states, "Quality counts more than quantity. While it's good to cultivate a diverse network of friends and acquaintances, you also want to nurture a few truly close friends who will be there for you through thick and thin." This also means the happier you are, the healthier you will be. There are medical studies that show happiness may also reduce the risk of heart disease. There is a strong link between health and happiness. Studies indicate that happy people have stronger immune systems, which means they are less likely to get colds, they recover more quickly from surgery, they cope better with pain, they have lower blood pressure, and they have a longer life expectancy than unhappy people. So you had better keep reading this book!

Choosing your friends is critical to a happy life. Being around brilliant people will make you more brilliant. Being around people who only skateboard will likely cause you to begin skateboarding. Being around better tennis players will help you to become a better tennis player. Being around a person who is a confident decision-maker will help you to become a better decision-maker. On the other side of the coin, choosing to be around people who do criminal acts will likely draw you down that same dark path. Choose your friends wisely. I chose a diverse set of friends. Some play chess, some paint, some have IT skills, and some love history. Being great at something takes a lot of practice at that something. Even those who have a spectacular gift at something still find the need to practice, perhaps for years, to attain greatness and remain great. If you have a passion for something, it won't feel like practice. It will feel like excitement. How many people could have been great at something but failed to try? They will never know what they don't know. Try new things. Simply begin them. If you don't start, you'll never know. Could you have been a great marksman, carpenter, pianist, language specialist, horticulturist, biologist, sculptor, distance runner, or swimmer? Could you be an expert in putt-putt golf, or a sunglass designer?

There is one more person who can get in your way of happiness, and that is yourself. It is critical that you are your best friend and greatest admirer. Be a friend to yourself, understand and believe you are of great value, and love who you are. Think back to when you were young and the fun you had with friends playing a game, riding bikes, fishing, throwing rocks, or camping. That young person is still you. It should be easier to figure out how to be happy as an adult than as a child because you have more knowledge and experiences. Is it, and if not, why not? You simply got off the path of a happy life. But you can get back on that youthful path at any age. Prove to yourself that you can lead a great and happy life. If you are having feelings of guilt, you must set them aside. You are only human. Each of us makes mistakes. We all understand that some mistakes are bigger than others. But here is the great news: the size of the mistakes (yes, even plural) does not matter. Forgive yourself. Do not drag guilt into your life because a marriage failed. Do not drag guilt into your life because you survived a military experience when others didn't. Do you drag guilt into your life because your car spun out of control and struck another car, harming someone else? Do not drag guilt into your life because you stole to get drugs. A bankruptcy does not lessen your individual value. Instead, simply start. Start with a first small step. Set a goal that will make you happier. You can get back on not just a good path but an amazing path. Perhaps a goal can be to join a choir. Try acting in a play. Learn how to paint. Learn how to skateboard. Learn how to swim. Try a zipline. Join a local ball club. Get back in great physical shape or run a marathon. The possibilities are endless. Guilt will harm you such that you will never reach the happiness each of us is meant to have. If you were at fault, then learn from the experience and ask for forgiveness. Maybe you will ask for forgiveness with a letter. Perhaps you will ask for forgiveness by directly talking with someone. If you are a person of faith you may ask for forgiveness in the form of prayer. But you must forgive yourself. Put the guilt behind you. Everyone makes mistakes. Sometimes we are simply in the wrong place at the wrong time when tragedy strikes. If you felt extreme guilt, it is only because you are a good person. I will repeat that: If you feel guilt, it is only because you are a good person. We also know that when you harm yourself, you harm others. A person who does not have any morals does not feel guilt. Thus that feeling of guilt means you are of good character. Understand that carrying your guilt objectively will help no one. Guilt cures nothing and will most certainly harm you. Set aside any stigma. Remember that you are of great value, and ask for help if you need it. In fact, ask for help even if you don't feel you need it. Asking for help is very rarely a bad thing. My hope is that in the future, you can then reach out and help someone else. In fact, perhaps you were meant to help many people. But you will never know unless you start healing yourself. Admit that you have a problem and take steps to find that amazing life.

If you have read this entire book, you know that one of the critical elements of happiness is helping others. Give someone the opportunity to help you. Not everything that has value can be counted. Things like love, compassion, kindness and caring. And not everything that truly counts finds a reward, except by those who do *that* everything which truly counts. Helping others will be its own reward. Go make yourself count by helping others. I promise you that helping others, even beginning with small acts of kindness, will bring you greater happiness.

There is also the need to forgive others who have caused you harm or distress. When forgiving is not possible, you need to instead focus on the positive experiences prior the incident. If you think that receiving a huge financial settlement to enrich yourself is going to make you feel happier the moment those funds hit your account, you are most certainly on the wrong path. Yet that is what society tries to teach us. Memories, such as the loss of a loved one, are not suddenly going to go away when your bank account is made larger. You have to instead try to forgive those that did you harm or, if you feel you are not capable of doing that at this time, focus on praising the time you had prior the incident or event. Focusing on the positive and forgiving those from the past are the only ways to sleep peacefully. You cannot change the past. When tragedy happens it usually effects many families. You will find that by reaching out to help others that are similarly hurting will also help you heal. This is also where compartmentalization may need to be practiced. Be thankful, not vindictive. Be thankful that you survived that car accident and not vindictive about the other driver. If you think you will be happier by being vindictive then you understand almost nothing about this book. Realize that when you hate you are effecting not only yourself but others around you. Also understand that if you are taking from someone else, being hurtful to someone else, you are also effecting others around them. Seek kindness, seek forgiveness. Be thankful that you are still healthy. Be thankful that the ones you care most about are also healthy so you have others to share your life with.

On the other side of the coin, when you are called upon to be a true friend, remember that listening is loving.

Chapter Four

Things around You and the Critical Elements to Happiness

I COULD GIVE YOU A cute adage that makes you think about happiness in life. Perhaps something like "Be understanding of your parents, never stop doing what you care most about, learn to use a semicolon, and seek love." But that is too flashy or abstract. That is not to say that I don't like that adage—I actually kind of do! But what I genuinely want to impart are true lessons. There is a well-known adage that is sometimes taught in philosophy classes, and it goes something like this.

There was a physics professor who had a wide, thick glass cylinder that was quite tall, and he placed it atop a table at the front of the lecture hall. Beside the tall glass cylinder were a lot of colorful big gemstones that appeared to be about golf-ball sized. The professor began the class by placing those gemstones into the cylinder until he could not fit any more. He added the gemstones until they came just beneath the uppermost plane of the cylinder. He then asked his students if they thought the cylinder was full. Of course many students sat quiet, as students tend to do, but those with some courage who were willing to participate in class to their own benefit shouted yes, the cylinder was full.

The professor gleefully told them they were wrong. What the students did not see was that the professor had a drawer in that table where he pulled out a smaller glass cylinder with smaller rough pebbles. He then proceeded to pour the rough pebbles into the tall cylinder while slightly shaking it, and the students witnessed the rough pebbles slipping between the open gaps and spaces formed between the much larger gemstones. The professor continued to pour the pebbles once again until they came just beneath the uppermost plane of the cylinder. As before, the professor asked if the cylinder was full. This time more students were willing to participate and shouted no. He told them they were right. That was when he opened another drawer and pulled out some exceptionally fine-grain sand. He shook the tall thick glass cylinder as he poured the sand into it. As before, the sand found its way between the gaps and spaces formed between the rough pebbles and between the golf-ball sized gemstones. The professor continued to pour the sand until it was just beneath the uppermost plane of the cylinder. He stepped back from the table and appeared to surrender with exhaustion from pouring as he asked the students if the cylinder was now in fact full. Some students said yes, and some said no. The professor smiled and said those who said no were correct. He pulled out yet another smaller glass cylinder filled with clear water. He then poured the water into the tall, thick glass cylinder until the water was just beneath the uppermost plane of the cylinder. The professor asked yet again, Is the cylinder full? Many students remained silent, but of those who participated, the majority said yes, the cylinder was full.

The professor then replied that indeed the cylinder was full. But now he asked another question. What did you learn from this demonstration? Some students said they learned that when you think you are done with a project, perhaps you should look at the project in other ways to determine whether that's really true. Another student said that when you think you are done with a project, you can always do more. And a third said he learned that he cannot always trust his conclusions. The professor interrupted the answers and surprised the students by stating that today's presentation was not regarding the subject of physics, to which the students were accustomed. Instead, it was a lesson about life. The things that were added to the cylinder were all parts of life. He said that if you want to live life to the fullest, you have to know what in life are the big gemstones. Once you figure those out, it is then that you can experience the finer things in life and bask in the water with a thirst for life. Know that there will be some rough pebbles along the way but that those rough pebbles are simply a part of life. In fact, if you live your life to its fullest, you will find the rough pebbles quite minor and unavoidable. So focus on the big gemstones, and don't worry about the rough pebbles. If, however, you mistakenly choose to focus on the rough pebbles first, you'll never be able to fit in the many big gemstones that life has to offer. And you may never recognize that even in rough-pebble times, you can experience the finest grains of sand and refreshing water. Even when things are getting you down, you can still stretch out your arms and walk into a spring rain shower to feel its refreshment. Thus, focus on the important things in life, the big things in life, the gemstones. Find the diamonds; they should always come first. Once you identify the gemstones, you will also be able to more greatly appreciate the many fine grains that will weave their way between those gemstones.

What value is that lesson unless you know what are the gemstones? It is especially important for you to understand that the term *stones* is in plural. The most joy-filled life, and thus the happiest life, requires many of the stones about to be discussed. In this chapter, I'll focus on the gemstones. In later chapters, I will discuss ways to avoid the rough pebbles. Having only one of the big gemstones is not enough for the happiest life. You will need at least four types of those gemstones: a lifelong partner, and secondarily your core of support; a passion; the ability to give; and, positive new experiences. In chapter 2, I expressed that likely the most important decision you will ever make in your life is finding the gemstone of a lifelong partner. That is the person who fully understands you, and you can talk to about literally everything. That is the person who cares more about your happiness than their own. That is the person who is truly joyful when you tell them you just won the lottery. That is the person who is genuinely happy when you passed that test to be a certified electrician. It is the person you can talk to about your most personal interests and desires. It is the person who will give you an organ if you ask them. Your core of support are those few individuals whom you can wholly trust, and thus they are a priority in your life.

Let me make this truly clear as part of the critical elements. The test of a true friendship is not the good times—it's the bad times. As an example, when everyone is making money in a business partnership, it is easy to continue the relationship. But what about when something unexpected happens with the business, and it is tested? What happens if one of the business partners is pulled away on a family emergency? What type of support are the other partners willing to provide, and for how long? You will be able to see people's true character only when they are going through hard times and being tested. Part of the critical elements is the sad but true understanding that you will not be loved unless you love others. Let me repeat that: You will not be genuinely loved unless you love others. When you hate, others can feel it unless you're an exceptionally good actor or a sociopath. Unless you love others, there will be very few people whom you can trust with your life to the truest meaning of that phrase. I have heard a saying that when you hold grudges, your hands are not free to catch blessings. I fully agree with that statement. Let me put this point in a more objective, practical, and clear manner. Whom would you trust today to disperse all your money should something happen to you? Can you be certain with 100 percent trust that the person would disperse the money exactly to your wishes and not to any of their interests? Whom would you trust to watch your pet when you have to go away on short notice and be certain that the caregiver will treat your pet as you would without charging you a dime? To whom would you hand the keys to your car without reservation and know that it will come back washed with a full tank of gas? To whom could you tell the most private of secrets and know that it will never go beyond you two? Most of us have very few people like that in our lives, and that is not a bad thing; it is a part of life. A person who has five trusted relationships does not mean that they are happier or better than a person who "only" has three trusted relationships. Get that thought out of your mind. People will move in and out of your life for various reasons. Maybe it's because of work, because of a relationship with someone else, or because of tragedy. The truly trusted person whom I refer to as your core of support is one of those people who absolutely loves you. That core of support individual will never be far away even if time separates you for an extended period. There is an old but well-proven fact that if you cannot trust people with small things, you certainly can't trust them with big things.

The point is that to be genuinely happy, you really shouldn't care what anyone else thinks except for those that love you. And those who truly love you simply want you immensely happy. Thus, live the life you want and do not ever make a decision based on what you think other people think, especially when those other people are thinking only about themselves and not your interests. You can truly only trust the people who genuinely love you to give you the true answer no matter what you think of the answer. And if you truly trust those people you'll objectively study that answer as being only in your interests. Let me make something also very clear about "trust". It is a two-way street. It means not only can you trust that individual to think about you and do the right thing, but that you can also trust that individual to trust in you. Let me give you an objective example. Let's say that Tom and Mary are dating. Mary is told by her "girlfriend" that she saw Tom hugging another woman. If Mary truly trusted Tom it would not bother her at all. She would ask Tom about it later without grave concern. Perhaps Tom was hugging the other woman because Tom just learned that her longtime pet had died and Tom knew that hugging the other woman, and telling her he understood the deep sadness for her loss, is something that she needed.

Perhaps the other woman confided in Tom that she was just diagnosed with cancer and she was frightened. She confided in Tom exactly because of his trusting character. After all, as Mary knew, Tom is a caring man and others understand that. Perhaps Mary's "girlfriend" was jealous of Tom and Mary's relationship and made up the story because she believed that she could cause trouble between them. Since this "girlfriend" did not understand what trust really means she didn't consider the possibility that the outcome of her telling this story will be losing Mary as a friend. Mary trusts Tom because she knows Tom truly loves her. He truly needs her. Just as she knows she needs him. They each know they do not have to guard against losing the other. That is one reason their love is so intense. There is no safety net needed. There is absolute trust. They have both fallen hard but they have fallen hard for each other. And that is a fabulous thing. That is the *wow* factor in a partner. That is part of an intense love. In life you will hopefully have a core of support as well as friends and acquaintances. A friend is one you interact with much more than just acquaintances. But to have the happiest life, you also need to pick your friends and acquaintances wisely. If you have to have a general rule for guiding you to finding someone who is more likely to become a close friend, then choose someone who is kind and emotional. Trust people who cry a lot. They are often of the best of character. Some say God gave men tears to tell others about their hearts.

What is meant by a gemstone being a passion? What form does it take? They are unique to you, and they will likely change as you go through life. They can be part of your work life or your private life and be in both. A *passion* may not be one thing that you are focused on but instead many small things. It may be a goal of gaining positive experiences no matter how small. It might be a great interest in ballet just as likely as sailing, or both. You might find you have a great interest in animals leading you on a path to become a veterinarian. Perhaps you love going to the rodeo and you'd like to try being a cowboy. It might be a love of opera just as likely as a love for hotrod drag races, or both. What you hope to find is a passion that can lead to your life's work.

Being able to work in a field that is your passion could be a great life. Let's say you love music, and you find work in a band or teaching others how to play. You like singing and find a job in public theater or writing musical scores. You like interviewing people and find a job in journalism. You love talking about your faith and you want to become a pastor. You love snow skiing, and you establish a company making skis or training downhill skiers. You love to cook and open a restaurant. You love magic and perform on stage. You had a parent with bad teeth, and you find dentistry very rewarding because you can help people like your parent. Being able to earn an income based on your passion can bring a lot of happiness. As a parent, you want to help your child identify a career path as early as possible so they can tie the two together.

As an individual, you want to continue to gain skills that can lead you to that desirable work position. But also realize that being passionate for whatever job you do is also great. In other words, be passionate for work itself. Find your passions in life. You are only harming yourself if you are negative about going to work. Do not think I *have* to go to work but think I *get* to go to work. Find the rewarding aspects of your work. Enjoying your job often revolves around your working environment and enjoying those with whom you work. But taking pride and being the best at what you do are great things and bring happiness. Although I don't have any statistic or mathematical model to rely upon, it is likely that the majority of people work in professions that are not their passion. But they use that employment to follow their passion after work. That is great so long as you continue to pursue a passion no matter your age. Having a passion is a critical element, so it is not surprising to learn that a person who does not have a passion is not as healthy and not as excited about life.

Find a passion, and you'll never work while doing it. As an engineer, I have found numerous things in life that I'd love to be a part of, but I can live only one life. I am an expert in construction, specializing in residential construction. I have always enjoyed doing all my own electrical work, plumbing, framing, trim carpentry, and HVAC repair.

The satisfaction of a job well done is very rewarding to me. I would love to have been an astronaut. I would love to design roller coasters. I love going fast, so the thought of being in a car race or road rally is exciting. I think it would be cool to work as an engineer who designs dramatic custom water features, like the Bellagio fountains in Las Vegas that make people stand in awe. I would love to design laser light shows and time them to music to enhance the experience. I learned how to fly a plane and got my private pilot's license. I got certified as an advanced open water and enriched air scuba diver. I constantly ask, "Can this be done better? Is this the best I can do?" If you do your best no matter what your job, I can assure you that you will be happier in life. I remember seeing *The Sound of Music* and immediately understanding the talent that Rogers and Hammerstein had in creating such a masterpiece. I immediately thought that it must have been difficult to leave the location, wherever they were creating this music, because of the excitement that must have been flowing through them like electricity. Those were amazing days, and it is unfortunate that so few of us can experience such a team effort. Working on such a team as a collaborative effort to accomplishing something so amazing is priceless. Imagine the excitement of being on a team that launches a rocket into space. Imagine the sensation of watching, hearing and feeling the launch. That is one of the joys of team sports. It would be a joy to even record the inventiveness as it was happening, to almost feel and see the genius as the music is being created, as the engine is being tuned, as the next idea is advanced.

If you wanted a list of things to be passionate about, there is no possible way for anyone to create a complete list. It is as boundless as there are personalities on this planet. At this time of my life, I have found a passion for finding great restaurants, great music, travel, and great movies. Of course I have a passion to make other's lives happier than mine, as well as to learn. Thus it is a dream, or perhaps a fantasy, that these words could be read by millions and that these words could hopefully resonate to improve the lives of those millions, and that those millions would talk to millions more. Currently I also have an interest in learning a new language. When I was younger, I had a passion to both waterski and snow ski. I also had a passion for swimming in addition to learning. When I was younger, my goal was to earn a college degree in engineering.

As I noted earlier, it is not uncommon for your passions to change as you pass through life. Maybe you're passionate about running, tennis, math, bird-watching, playing the violin, learning about world history, learning how to develop a network protocol, understanding mechanical devices, or riding a bike. Maybe you are passionate about flowering plants, annuals, or plants that thrive in a humid climate versus those that like a wet environment. Maybe you love fishing, whether it is ocean fishing, freshwater fishing, fly-fishing, or noodling. Maybe you have a passion to excel in the game of golf, bocce ball, or chess. Maybe you have a passion to learn how to pilot a plane. You want to learn how to ride a horse and go camping. You want to learn more about chemistry. Perhaps you found a passion for art such as watercolors, glass-cutting, sculpting, or photography. Perhaps your interest in photography is landscapes or catching the aurora borealis. Maybe your passion is learning about cameras themselves. Maybe you're an inventor. As you get older, perhaps you'll seek a job photographing food for restaurants in your local area. Seek a job as a flight instructor. Sell artwork at a local festival. Maybe during your lifetime you've discovered a passion for wines, and you are going to open a business giving wine tours to different regions around the world. Perhaps you have a passion to see every national park in the country or to visit every professional baseball stadium. My hope is that you have not just one passion but several. Having a goal and a dream is a critical element of living an incredibly happy life. Thus if you find that you're watching too much television or spending too much time on the computer, simply stop doing these things. It's never too early in life to start a new passion. And perhaps more important, it's never too late in life to start a new one either.

What is meant by a gemstone being the ability to give? This does not mean money. As a reminder, this book is about happiness. Thus the use of the term *give* is meant to mean happiness to others. You will find that bringing joy or happiness to others, helping others, is extremely rewarding to you. In fact, it is critical to your happiness.

A child in a hospital who is visited by a pet isn't excited just to see the dog. The child is not happiest sitting in bed while the dog is sitting at the door several feet away. No, the child wants to put their arms around the dog, touch the dog, and pet the dog. Why is that? Because a child intuitively feels the joy of reaching out and being kind. They want to pet the dog because they know a dog would like that. That is why a petting zoo is much more enjoyable for a child than a zoo where one can only see the animals. The same is true for all of us, whether you think of it objectively or not. There are times when you might want some alone time because of life's events. But in general you will be happier sitting in a room with others than sitting alone. You will be happier when you reach out to touch another person rather than standing at arm's length. Imagine how different a child would be if it was left in a bassinet without being touched versus being held in loving arms each day. Reaching out is also a lesson for adults. In fact when you are feeling alone in life you can find a cure to that loneliness by reaching out and helping someone else. If would be very difficult to feel alone when you are tying the shoes of a child, teaching a friend how to hula hoop or tutoring a student in math. I read once that the secret to your next job is with the person you have not met yet. You're not going to get great opportunities from just being around the same people. Hence another reason to reach out to others is to learn about something you don't know. That "weak connection" at the sandwich shop or at the mailbox could take you on a totally new and exciting path in life. Here are a few more examples of ways to improve your day if you're not feeling motivated or needed. Reach outward and stop thinking inward. It's almost impossible to be unhappy when you're helping someone fix a leaking kitchen faucet. It's almost impossible to be unhappy when you're reading to a person with poor eyesight. It's almost impossible to be unhappy when you're helping a child in an after-school program to read and when you're helping a neighbor plant flowers.

Helping others brings happiness. Think of the third critical element of this chapter, which is giving. Do you know the poorest school in your area? Find out where it is located and go talk to the principal to see what she needs. Befriend someone old or someone who has lost someone. They will have too much pride to say they are lonely, but stay and ask questions. If you walk with them, try to find a memorable location, and try to play music from their generation so they can remember that visit each time they hear that song.

Here's another example. Let's say you have what others perceive as an amazing life because you have extreme wealth. You have the ability to go out every day on your yacht and drink champagne for six hours before you return to the dock. Now, let's suppose you had no friends. How many times could you leave the dock for six hours and feel fulfilled and excited? Even such an amazing life would get boring. If you add different friends every day, it may prolong the excitement such that you could go out for a few more days. But that is only if you knew that those you took out on your yacht were people who were genuinely appreciative of the amazing experiences you were providing them. If the "friends" were actually the type who talk behind your back, then the total experience of having them on your yacht would not be a good experience. A person who is a "friend" is not one who gets on board and acts like the cruise is nothing because you are rich. The measure of good character is the person who gets on board understanding that they could never afford this luxury themselves, and they sincerely appreciate the gift. It is the guest who asks if they can be of help in any manner to not only you but also the crew. They are the guests who you can see are genuinely enjoying the gift you are providing via your hospitality. But even with friends of great character on board, you could feel fulfilled and excited only for a limited period of time. Now, let's change our scenario even more and say that on your way to your yacht, you arrive immediately after a horrible car crash and see a person injured on the side of the road needing assistance. I would certainly hope you would recognize that life would feel much more rewarding by helping that person instead of proceeding to your yacht. Most of us seek happiness every day, but to be genuinely happy, you also need to feel needed. Many of us get the feeling of being needed by our work, family or friends or a combination thereof. It is likely that five years into the future, the yacht owner will not be able to remember very many specific days on that yacht with friends. However, he'll likely remember for the rest of his life the gift of being in the right place at the right time to help that injured person on the side of the road. That is the ability to give.

There are many stories I have read or been told of that remain in my mind because of acts of kindness and those that give of themselves in the stories. And stories of kindness, quite frankly, make me feel happier. This first story is about a delivery driver. Her name is Amanda. Amanda stopped to deliver two packages at a house on her route, and the lady who lived there happened to be out checking the mailbox. She and Amanda struck up a conversation as Amanda walked the packages to the front door. Amanda asked if the woman had enjoyed the holidays. The woman was incredibly open and answered with the truth. "He's sick. My husband's sick. He has cancer." This statement shocked Amanda, and she did not know what to say other than to politely change the subject. But as she pulled away from the lady's house, Amanda could not get the woman's heartache out of her mind. "My heart's pounding. I do probably twenty more stops, and I have to go back," Amanda said. Amanda, as a delivery driver, was on a tight schedule and had to make deliveries. But her priorities changed that day. Amanda turned around and went back to the house. "I stopped what I was doing. I went back to that neighborhood and rang her doorbell," Amanda explained. "She came down the stairs, and she had tears in her eyes when she saw it was me. She smiled, and I said, 'Ma'am, can I pray with you?' And she just broke down. She came out on the front porch and squeezed me so tight." She prayed with the grieving woman; it was the compassion the lady needed. Amanda, who is a religious person, is quoted as saying, "I pray every day for the Lord to use me." Clearly on that day, she was rewarded. That is the ability to give.

There is a woman who went to a well-known grocery store in Alvin, Texas. She went to pick up her daughter's birthday cake. When she tried to pay for her cake, the bakery staff informed her it had already been paid for. She said, "Wait, like somebody that I know, like their grandmother or something?" The grocery store employee said, "No, they left a note." The handwritten note read, "My son Nehemiah would have been eight years old today. I want to remember my son by doing good to others. I hope you enjoy your child's cake, and I hope your day is special. Hold your baby a little tighter today, watch them as they play, be patient with them, kiss their sweet little hand, and tell them how much you love them. Our children are such special gifts. I hope your day is beautiful. Much love from me and my angel in heaven to your family." That is the ability to give.

I read a story about a family of five, with two twin boys aged twelve and a younger sister barely a year old. Their mom worked days, their dad worked nights, and they both spent their time off trying to take care of three cranky, hungry children. The power and electricity were shut off at regular intervals because of the parents' inability to pay the bills. One of the twin boys, to this day, remembers one time in the winter just after the power was shut off, there was a knock on the door. His mom went to answer it, and she came back into the house crying with an envelope in her hands. He and his twin brother thought at that young age that it was a letter telling them that they had to leave the property. But it turned out that it was an envelope filled with money. His mom still talks about the stranger who left it because she swears that they wouldn't have made it through the winter without it. That is the ability to give.

"When I was about five in the mid-1970s, I was sitting on one of the mechanical horses that rock back and forth outside of a Woolworth's and playing while I was waiting for my mom, who was in the store. Some lady walked by and put a quarter in to make it go. I was over the moon. It is a moment of pure joy that I've remembered vividly. I still even remember what that glorious stranger looked like." That is the ability to give.

"I got the heart-wrenching call that my twenty-six-year-old brother had passed suddenly the night before. Two days before that, I had broken my right ankle badly, thus preventing me from driving the six hours back to my hometown. I got to the airport and ... I sort of collapsed into my chair and tried my best to hold it together in public. Without a word, the elderly woman next to me reached over and held my hand. She didn't say anything ... just held my hand. It was the nicest gesture from a stranger who knew I was about to fall apart." That is the ability to give.

"I was really depressed after having a baby, started a new job. I was having a hard time catching on to how the return system worked and had a really impatient customer who was getting snappy with me. I was still really emotional and started crying. The next customer in line left the store, and I thought she was upset too. But she came back with cookies. She went and bought me cookies. And I just started crying all over again." That is the ability to give.

"When I was about twelve years old, I went to a bookstore with my cousins. We bought a few books and then went outside and started reading them. We were getting stared down by this old man, but after about ten minutes of him staring at us, he got up off the bench and went inside the bookstore. He later came out about five minutes later with three gift cards. He walked up to us with a smile and said, 'I love seeing kids read,' and he handed each of us a twenty-dollar gift card. I have never been so shocked and touched." That is the ability to give.

These are examples of what I meant when I stated in chapter 1, "When you are given that gift of being at the right place and at the right time, don't just consider helping—objectively act."

Let us return to our philosophy lesson. What are some of the objective ways to know whether a person is really one of those amazing people who may be your core of support? One of the first steps is actually considering that question. It is a good thing to recognize that sharing your life with special people is incredibly rewarding. You will feel that goodness in your inner core. So it is a good thing to actually ask the question throughout your life: "Am I a person of such character that others would consider me as their core of support?" It is also fair to ask the question if this person you're conversing with really cares about your happiness. Listen objectively to that person. Is that person asking about you, or is that person telling you only about himself or herself? If that person is asking about you and asking how he or she can make your day better, then you may be speaking to someone who can be part of your core of support. Time and experiences will help you with that decision. But also realize that relationships are a two-way street. You have to objectively consider who you are. Those who are kind will attract others who are kind. Those who are coarse will attract others who are coarse. I promise you that if you take true steps to be kind to others, you will be happier. And when I say true steps, I mean firsthand kindness.

Examples of firsthand kindness include telling someone in the parking lot that they left their lights on inside their car. Helping a parent with a toddler in a stroller to carry the stroller up a set of steps. Covering a person with your umbrella when the rain unexpectedly starts. Holding the door open for another person. Anonymously paying for the cup of coffee for the person behind you in line. Leaving money at your local restaurant to be used for the first family who arrives with a parent in uniform. Taking in the trashcans of a neighbor or mowing their lawn while they are away. Helping the elderly neighbor with an electrical problem or cleaning their windows. Leaving a kind letter in the mailbox for the mail person even when it's not a holiday. The list is endless. The fact is that these gestures can be small. But you will find that even small gestures are rewarding for you as well as for the person receiving the kindness. I make it a point, a kind of pledge to myself (although it comes naturally), to reach out to at least one person every day with an act of kindness. Sometimes I have only the opportunity to tell someone how cute their earrings are or how pretty a smile they have. Sometimes it is a joke, asking the jogger next to me to slow down so that I look better if someone is watching. But these moments are still important. They are important to me and, I believe, to those I make smile or help. Imagine if we all made that pledge.

When I say true steps, I am not referring to giving money. This is not about writing a check to some organization, if you are fortunate enough to have that financial ability. Writing a check is quite often just an illusion of doing good. If you want true and lasting change in a person or neighborhood, you should look to donate your time and energy first. It might feel good to write a check to a nationally recognized organization, but that check might not truly affect a single individual. That is unfortunately an objective reality. If you want to make a true difference with a financial donation, consider making the donation to a local organization first, where you actually witness their work. Equally important and rewarding is signing up to do some local community work. I learned not to invest in companies unless I understood what that company actually does, and that type of financial investment has worked out very well for me. There is no reason not to apply objective criteria to charities. I would not invest in a company because it is the hot company on TV. That is also true about my purchase of a product such as a car or cell service. I objectively evaluate each product for my needs and not what is advertised in all the different media. You have to realize that as a consumer, you are constantly bombarded with advertising. In many instances, you do not even know it. There may be stories you read that are actually sponsored stories or advertisements. The story might be about a fabulous hotel on some gorgeous island. All of it can be an advertisement. Do you realize there are people on the internet who are labeled influencers? They are paid by others to create content to affect your purchasing decisions. It might be a really handsome man drinking a specific vodka and implying it makes his life amazing. Or perhaps it's a beautiful girl approaching a man because of the car he is driving. The marketing is endless. Therefore you should first establish criteria for what you need before you purchase. The same holds true for charities. You should first establish the facts of where each dollar of a donation goes before you donate. When you learn about the great things these local charities are doing to make a difference, it will increase your happiness in donating those funds or working with those charities. Isn't that a lot more rewarding than seeing an advertisement or hearing from word of mouth and simply sending money?

Do not weigh yourself down with what others think. Realize the true meaning of this. When I say others, there is an imaginary scale on which to assign importance. On one end of the scale are likely your parents or family members, and on the other end of the scale are complete strangers. You may recognize this as kind of an honor scale, meaning those who love you the most should be most important to you. But at the same time, those who absolutely love you—and I mean unconditionally love you—are not going to be lost by the decisions you make or the passions you discover. That's what true love is. Your mom is not going to love you less because you choose to be an actor and barely make a living, just as she is not going to love you more if you suddenly become a famous actor. As I stated earlier, the test of true love is not the good times; it's the bad times. My true wish is that in your life, you will maintain some remarkably close friendships. But my ultimate wish is that you find true love, are able to find passions in your life, find daily excuses to be kind and enjoy limitless positive new experiences. My wife will tell you that I am a sucker for a good love story. There is a line in the movie *Hitch*: "Life is not the number of breaths you take—it's the moments that take your breath away." May your breath be stolen by true loves, true passions, kindness to others and amazing experiences.

What exactly is meant by a gemstone being positive new experiences? First of all the term "positive" is a perception. Sometime things will happen to you that you will not recognize as being positive. A person who understands the critical elements of happiness will look at almost all of their experiences in life in a positive manner. But what I mean by this fourth gemstone is for you to seek out new experiences. And it is critical that you do this through your entire life. A person who is coming to the end of their life is not going to look back and think they had an amazing, happy and fulfilling life because of the material things they acquired. That person will look back and think of all the amazing experiences and loves they had that actually created the amazing life. A goal for a great and happy life is not to acquire material things but to experience multiple things. Reconsider buying that new couch and instead spend the money on that trip to a national park. You'll never regret it.

It is through new experiences that you will likely find a passion that will greatly interest you and enhance excitement and happiness in your life. Once you find your first passion do not stop seeking positive new experiences. New experiences will always add to whatever passions you find. Happiness is directly tied to positive experiences. It should be a priority to seek out new experiences. You can objectively understand this by simply re-arranging the furniture in your room or changing the paint color. These changes are a new stimulation to you and thus you will feel better about that room. The same is true on a much broader scale in life. If you do the same thing every day you will find life much less exciting. The simple step of changing your routine at least one day a month, for your entire life, to do something totally new to you will bring you greater joy. Don't drive that same route home from work. Instead turn right and find a location to view the sunset. Do not watch that same television program. Instead go watch a local theater group perform a play. Perhaps you can sign up for a cooking class and watch a youth baseball game. Maybe you can go talk to a group of older adults at a local assisted living center and learn about their lives.

When I say positive new experiences I don't just mean trying tennis, swimming, golf and archery although these are included on the list. What I truly mean is to strive for things that excite all your senses as well as small things. Strive to visit other countries and try new foods, new music, new cultures. Have you ever tried a zip-line or a roller coaster? Try experiencing a country band, opera, jazz concert as well as a symphony. Learn what excites you. Try Chinese, Indian, Mexican and Mediterranean restaurants or dishes. Try a massage or pedicure or just a new hair style. Stay up late and seek out the best place for a sunset and then stay until you witness a shooting star. Try getting up early and watch a sunrise when the sky is clear. Seek out watching the Northern Lights. Try the new experience of visiting a different national park in your country or another country. Try a cruise or a train ride. Try new experiences no matter the degree or level at least once a month. Maybe the new experience will only be trying to learn to ice skate or ice fish. Perhaps it will be trying painting with watercolors or drawing with colored pencils. The list is endless. But understand that sitting on a couch day after day will not bring you happiness like getting off that couch and trying something new. Spending all your time on a cell phone or computer will not bring you happiness like putting the cell phone away and going on a hike. Seeking new experiences or new goals is critical to happiness. And if you don't have a lot of money to try new experiences that is just an excuse. As an example, go to your local library and ask the librarian for a book about adventure. She will likely laugh because the library is filled with thousands of adventures. No matter where you live a book can literally take you away just as a great movie. You will forget where you are. You will forget any real-world concerns. Reading a great book can take you to places that you can only imagine and allow you to discover new things. Reading to a child is especially important because it can bring up very meaningful conversations. This is also true about going to the playhouse to see a play or going to the theater to see a movie. Bring your child to a movie you love, such as the Sound of Music (if it is ever re-released) in a theater. Perhaps you have a favorite holiday movie you can watch together every year. You will create a memory for yourself and hopefully your child that you both will never forget. There are many times in life that you live through an experience and you don't think much of it. Like bringing your child to a fabulous movie. The memory may be brushed from your mind like a stranger in a crowd. But many years in the future you'll look back and think about that moment. Sometimes we just don't recognize some of the most significant moments of our lives. This is especially true if that memory includes someone you suddenly lost. If you understand the critical elements of happiness you'll not only try to create more of those moments for yourself but also for others you care about. That is an amazing and happy life. Hold your mom's hand just a little longer next time. Squeeze your dad a little harder when you give him that hug and tell him how much you love him. Even better, take a specific trip to your parent's house only to tell them about all the great memories you had of growing up and be specific about the memories. I understand that we all likely have some memories that don't bring joy and laughter. Forget about them. They will not benefit you or anyone else. Since a happy life is one that brings immediate memories of those experiences to mind, what was exciting about last week? What lasting memory do you have about last month?

As a final note in this chapter, I would say you should live life as young as you can. Think young. When you stop feeling young is not when you grow old, you grow old when you start thinking that you can no longer feel young. Imagine. Feel that feeling of happiness and freedom when you maintain a mindset where you notice that "What the hell?" is always the right decision. You only live once. Don't you want to try your best to get it right, to make it all worth it?

Chapter Five

Tools for a Happier Life: How to Create Amazing Days

ONE OF THE SUGGESTIONS OF this book is for you to buy a really nice calendar with room to write on it. A true paper calendar is best, but if you choose to use a calendar on your computer, that is fine. Hang the calendar up in an area where you can view it every day. You will also need a journal to actually record a list. By *record*, I prefer handwritten, but I am certainly not against storing your notes on a computer if that is easiest for you. This list will eventually make its way onto that calendar, because that calendar is going to become your amazing-day calendar.

Each year you'll create a new list and buy a new calendar. It's a great tradition to start off the new year. You will likely be transferring some of the prior list to the new list and new calendar at the beginning of the year. I suggest that you may want to keep and store those prior calendars to look back at those memories on a year-by-year basis at some later date. The list is going to be created by you and will include things big and small, new and old, unique and common. For ease of discussion, let's call your list parts of your plan. Each of your plans is ideally going to be part of an amazing day. Sometimes your plan will be only half of an amazing day. Sometimes your plan will be an amazing hour. Or your plan may be limited to fifteen minutes. Perhaps the fifteen minutes include a phone call you get from your tearful daughter, who is in college and is incredibly happy to receive the care package you sent. Because you tracked it by FedEx, it included a surprise hug from her best friend (whom you worked with for the surprise) because you couldn't be there. The surprise care package also included dinner out for your daughter and a friend, as well as a video of you and her favorite pet. In the video, you are lip-synching to one of her favorite songs to bring her a smile.

A goal is to get as many parts of your plan on that calendar as reasonably possible. You are going to be transferring part of your plan onto specific days of your calendar. And you want to enact at least part of your plan as often as possible. Thus the calendar is for recording the actual date in the future where you are going to experience something you're looking forward to. There is nothing wrong with coming up with a great plan—in other words a great day—and repeating it. Thus your calendar is going to be filled as much as possible with future things that you want to experience. You need to put every element of that plan, which is built from elements on your list, somewhere on a future calendar date within a reasonable period of time. Things that are simple can be put on the calendar within a few days or weeks—for example, a picnic or a movie. Things like concerts or plays might be scheduled ahead a month or two. That amazing vacation might be two years away. Give each a specific date. Also important is to be specific with the elements of your list that create your plan. Always try to prioritize getting elements of your plan, which is created from your list, onto your calendar. The sooner, the better. Live today. It is important to understand that a goal without a plan is just a wish. Get busy living. Happiness is a journey, not a destination you can plan to reach at a later date. There is a saying that every man dies, but not every man truly lives. Thinking of those words can help you during the day to make decisions to improve your life and make it more meaningful, thus making yourself happier. If you understood the critical element "the ability to give," those things to "improve your life" may be in fact directed toward making someone else's day better. The end result would be not only you happier but adding happiness to someone else's day. What would make you happier: planting some flowers at your house, or perhaps going to see your mom with flowers and planting them at her house? As I mentioned earlier, do not take things for granted in your life. The more you take for granted, the less you will appreciate those things. Time may not be your friend in life. None of us know exactly when our lives will end. You will never regret doing something you enjoy now versus delaying that experience. I will repeat a quote I enjoy from educator Claude Bissell, who wrote, "Risk more than others think safe, care more than others think is wise, dream more than others think is practical."

Remember that your goal is to create an amazing day. So you need to begin recording in your list positive things of each day. If you have never taken the time at the end of the day to focus on the positive parts of your day, you will begin to understand the true benefit of doing so. Although this sounds simple, this first slight change in your life can actually lead to experiences that are quite amazing. It is equivalent to the person who loses fifty pounds. If you speak to that person about losing that amount of weight, they will tell you about the many changes they experienced by losing those fifty pounds. They have more energy, sleep better, feel more self-confident, have a different attitude toward life, and have a better self-image. Yet before that person lost the fifty pounds, they could not imagine all those other significant changes they would experience. It's never just a simple statement of "Yeah, I lost fifty pounds." Thus, I cannot tell you exactly how different your life is going to be by changing your focus at the end of each day. But if you begin to focus on the positives of your day, which will be discussed further, I promise you a significant change for the better. It may even be a change for you to recognize those many positive things, some of which you took for granted. One simple change is to promise yourself, or make it a rule in your family that each day must start with a positive comment. You will see that it can be quite fun when you catch someone making the first comment as a negative one and correcting them. You will notice a greater happiness with these two simple changes. When you get home record the positive things of the day, and, when you start your day start with a positive comment.

With your journal, you are going to record positive list items. You want to record them at least at the end of the day. But I am certainly not against taking moments of time here or there when you're inspired to do so. This is consistent with the concept of when you're on vacation to write down all that happened each day of your vacation in a journal. This journal writing system brings back that great day even while on vacation. It's a great way to spend every dinner while on vacation. And remember that these are also shared memories if you're with family or friends. That will add to the experience of everyone on the vacation. Of course, you can always keep your own vacation journal with private memories, if you wish. Both systems provide a technique to vividly relive that great vacation any time you wish in the future, perhaps while scanning those limited number of pictures from the vacation. In fact, you may be using your vacation journal in the future as part of an amazing day when you choose to reread it, perhaps while on a picnic. When you write on your calendar, you should choose a standout color that is bright and positive. Thus your goal is to have a very brightly colored calendar by the end of the year. This calendar is going to become a place where you can quickly see a list of future goals, future dreams, future aspirations, and equally important and amazing events and days. Let me repeat that: a calendar only of the good things. I am going to discuss later the need to compartmentalize and forget the negative. There is no benefit to remembering the negative, just as there is no benefit to worrying. I will make an absolute statement that worrying will never benefit you and does not change anything. In the same regard, panicking will never benefit you. If you worry about the mortgage getting paid, does it suddenly get paid? If you worry that the bus will be late, does that cause the bus to arrive? If you worry about falling off the ladder, does that add confidence to your stability on that ladder? I will repeat: there is no benefit to worrying. Equally, panicking never helps you. Panicking is worse because it could be the actual cause of something tragic. If you panic while driving a car, is the likely outcome going to be better? If you panic in an emergency situation, such as trying to help someone during a medical emergency, is the result a better outcome? I will repeat that you must learn to not panic—and the key word is *learn*. It is education and experiences that will help you objectively overcome panic. Education and experience are equivalent to putting a plan in place for safety and proper action, just like a firefighter practicing putting out a staged fire before experiencing a real one.

When there is a perceived stressful situation in the future, you are going to have to learn to not worry. Part of the critical elements of happiness is to learn to cross bridges when you get to them. But you also need to be a decision-maker when you get to that bridge so you can put that matter behind you; more on this later. For now, you need to start focusing on positive things. These are the positive things that will get on your list, and when combined, they can become part of your plan. If your plan is lengthy enough, it will become an amazing day.

The positive things can come from any of your senses. The ideal positive "thing" is quite likely something that excites all of your senses at once. They can be visual, audible, taste, smell, touch, and most likely a combination of many. You want to write down those elements that can create a fabulous day in detail. Some of the elements that you will be recording will be bits and pieces of a combination of nice elements of a day. An example may be riding your bike on a great park trail. I encourage you to think about all of your senses; be detail oriented. I suggest music and foods that you'll bring along. Include the time of day, a blanket and utensils for the picnic, the location to view the best sunset, and more. If you have music as part of your picnic be aware of others around you and do not disturb them. Some other positive things may be bringing along a backpack full of picnic supplies to a great picnic area. Listen to music while people-watching along a riverbank. Follow your local area's "things to do" advertisements to catch local bands in a nearby park. Be a volunteer to an animal shelter and meet the cutest animal ever.

Let's say that you're driving to work, and you see someone on a sailboat in the water. You think it would be great to take sailing lessons. That should be part of your list. You also go to lunch and meet a really nice person in line, and have a good sandwich. You should make it a point to ask the person in line their name and focus on remembering it. Learning to remember other people's names is another goal you should have. You'll have a much happier experience addressing someone by their name, and they'll feel better about you for knowing their name. It's a genuinely nice lesson to learn and another tiny piece of the critical elements to add to not only your happiness but also the happiness you can bring to others.

Let me give you two simple scenarios regarding the simple task of ordering a sandwich at your local deli. In the first scenario, you simply wait in front of the counter each Monday as the staff member prepares your sandwich. You take your sandwich, leave, and eat alone in your office. You never chat with anyone at the deli. You simply order, wait for your sandwich, and leave. In the second scenario, you ask the person preparing your sandwich their name. Each Monday, you chat a little more and learn both your children go to the same school. How much better is your experience at the deli by having those conversations versus simply waiting for your order? It is not only kind to learn someone's name, but it also can add to a happier day. Plus, a positive thing of remembering people's names is that it is a great brain exercise! It's another small piece on a list that has many pieces, and it will create that positive experience. It's simply polite to call people by their name. If you go to the same sandwich shop, try to learn the names of the employees who serve you, and make sure to say hello. Do you know the name of the man who works at the local gas station? It would be nice for you to say hello to him as well. It will benefit both of you. How about the cashier at your grocery store? They have a nametag for a reason. Say hello to those folks as well. It's "just" another act of kindness. Your list can actually be endless, and that is an exceptionally good thing. Having a longer list means that you are objectively finding more positive things in your life! It would be sad to meet a person who cannot think of things to put on a list.

When you get home, you'll write down the name of the person you met in line, the name of the sandwich place, and the really good sandwich. You now know that you can return to the sandwich place with someone you care about to share that really good sandwich, or maybe you can meet up with the person you met in line. In fact you can introduce your mom to the employees at the sandwich shop when you bring her. I assure you that your mom is going to remember that sandwich shop visit in a much more positive way then simply buying a sandwich in the usual manner.

Another critical element to happiness is that you should try to improve the life of at least one person you interact with during a given day. When I say improve, I mean adding something positive. It can be quite minor; it may be complimenting someone on their hairstyle. It may be opening a door for someone. It may be letting someone borrow your reading glasses. It may be telling someone a cute joke that you know. The list is endless. The hope is that you'll receive a smile for your efforts. When I say efforts, I do not mean that it takes something from you to do this act of kindness. In fact, the effort that you take will be returned to you in the feeling of happiness that you'll recognize. Yes, kindness feels like happiness. It's just a directional thing. As kindness flows out of you, you'll find happiness flowing back in. You can't do this to everyone you interact with because then it becomes fake. It won't feel real to you, and if it isn't real to you, then it won't be real to that person. If you are actually thinking about this in an objective manner at the beginning of the day, then you should consider the person who seems most alone to be the person you chat with. For example, maybe you could give a compliment to a shy person in the elevator. Maybe you could help the elderly woman at the grocery store push her cart, and you can learn about her life for the next few minutes. Maybe you can pay it forward and purchase those groceries for the family that arrived at the grocery store in a car that is on its last legs.

You will also recognize that with experience, you can look back at old calendars or old plans and put together items to create an amazing day by revisiting great prior places. Perhaps it will begin with another walk in the park like the one last June, when the tulips just began to blossom. Then it will continue with photographing birds like last March. Then you'll go to that great sandwich place and have that great sandwich. Then you'll rent bikes like last September and go hear that free band near city hall, where you'll picnic near the fountain. Because this picnic is a new location, you'll be sure to also record the exact location in your list. And as the sun begins to set, you'll be in that location that captures the best sunset. Or perhaps you'll move your location, at the time of sunset, to get the greatest view from atop a building, or on a riverbank where you can see the horizon unimpeded. Perhaps one of your calendar plans will be, "Experience the best sunset from atop the waterfront warehouse loft patio." Again, your goal is to create as many of these amazing days as you can. But don't try too hard, unless you find this new activity of designing the perfect day fun in itself. This activity also takes balance. Perhaps starting with organizing an amazing day just once a month is achievable before you try making each weekend fabulous.

As a reminder, one of the building blocks to a great life is living amazing days. I find it easiest to plan for amazing days by creating a list of great experiences to formulate a plan to fill that amazing day. I chose to objectively focus on amazing days because each day starts anew. If one specific day does not work out to be the best, you always have tomorrow! So even though I chose the period of a day, because they are so easy to reset given a night's rest, I strongly encourage you to focus on creating as many plans as possible in any given week. For example, plan an amazing morning for Saturday morning, or perhaps a great lunch on Wednesday, or perhaps a great half-day getaway on the fifteenth. Those can all be amazing moments, or perhaps extraordinary. My hope is that you are including someone to join you in most of your plans on a regular basis. If you want to think of a way to prioritize your amazing days, you should look to the future. My hope is that you will begin to realize that you can, with practice, create some amazing, lasting-memory days. The goal is to actually outdo yourself. Maybe your first amazing day plan was based on seeing a local play. Your second amazing day can build upon that experience and now be a picnic on a fabulous vista followed by a local band performance in a park. The third amazing day can be a combination of inviting over your parents for a game of cards plus wine-tasting, followed by a movie at home that you know they will enjoy. Remember that when creating an amazing day, you want to consider all of your senses: taste, smell, touch, sound, and sight. When you have your parents over, you may want to have cookies freshly baked and fresh flowers on the table when they arrive, as well as some music your dad enjoys on the speaker.

Notice that I used the phrase "memory making." What do I mean by that? Well, let's assume for a moment that you are coming to end of your life, and now you're looking back. With the knowledge of this book, you know that you had an amazing life. But as you look back, what are those moments that rise to the top? I certainly could not imagine anyone who reads this book would look back and think, "I'm really proud I made every mortgage payment on time," or, "I was never late with an assignment in school." Those things are not about happiness. My true hope is that you had a life of extraordinary things. Thus your lasting memories include things that you cannot explicably plan. The extraordinary memories include experiences such as the birth of your first child or perhaps the excitement of winning that big game. But if you truly practice what is in this book, then I may have a hand in creating some of your extraordinary memories—ones where you take an amazing day to an extraordinary day. Hopefully you'll be able to look back with pictures and journals to see those picnics in the park when the tulips were blooming. The vacation in Europe where the couple sitting next to you mentioned how happy you two looked together. The balloon ride where you toasted with champagne that the last child was out of the house, and a new chapter in your life was beginning. The birthday party you held for your daughter, who is now a veterinarian, at the zoo, where she had hugged a lamb. The camping trip with pictures of the fishing, canoeing, roasting of marshmallows, and the horseshoe-toss trophy being awarded to mom. Perhaps you may even have the calendars to prove it. Start practicing with smaller plans created from your list of positive things you've now recognized. With practice, you'll be able to create some amazing days filled with plans you've created, taking into account all of your senses.

I also want to make the point that to live an amazing life, you certainly don't need to wait until you are old and gray before you ask questions that can lead to that happier life. Here is a great question to determine whether you're living life to the fullest: How much did you love? By that, I mean how much did you love all facets of your life? The greatest happiness in life is to love and be loved. The two biggest questions are likely regarding your work and your life partner. Did you love your work? How many times did you express passion to your partner? A key to life is finding the things you love: people, work, interests, smells, food, views, and things that make you feel passion. Find as many things as possible that you're passionate about, and you can't help but have a fabulous life. Part of the fun of life is the act itself of finding things that you're passionate about. You're certainly not going to find them by sitting on the couch or viewing social media. This is another one of those times when I say you don't know what you don't know. So try new things! Different is a good thing. If you don't do something different today, then yesterday will be the same as today, and that will be repeated tomorrow. Your life will be a repeat of yesterdays. Make a positive effort to try something new. How about rearranging the furniture in a room? You may find that you like the change. Try tennis, bike riding, puzzles, scuba diving, hot sauces, classical music, a change in hairstyle, different shoes, going to the movies, going out to a park, staring at the sky to find a shooting star, camping in the backyard— the possibilities are endless. Discovering new things in life can bring happiness. Try riding a two-person bike. Try painting with watercolors. Try a foreign movie. Try a balloon ride. Try ziplining. Try canoeing. Try picnicking. Try changing your evening wear. Try something new in the bedroom. Change your routine by going home a different way. Try a new restaurant on the first of every month. Go away for the weekend to a new town every third month. Take lessons to ride a motorcycle. Take lessons to learn the harmonica or the piano. Try yoga. Learn a magic trick. Plant something beautiful in your garden. Clean up the street and sidewalk along your block. Again, this list is endless. Trying something new does not mean that you have to do this every week. Maybe it will be once a month. Maybe it will be every day for a solid month. Maybe it will be on your next vacation. Start imagining and start living life by adding color to your calendar. That would be an exceptionally good thing. Get away from routine. Change a room around and see how nice it feels. Go to a movie on Tuesday.

Why wait? Why wait to send out that resume? If you have read this book you know that not getting the job is not a bad thing. All of us have been passed over for a job or not had a project approved that we supported. You can learn from sending out that resume what you may need to change to get that future job. Failing to try is failing. Why wait to travel to that place you've always wanted to go? At least ask the question of why you are delaying that action. Of course, there may be true instances where waiting is something you have to do for factual reasons. Happiness is a journey, not a destination you can plan to reach at a later date. If you can't create a complete amazing day, you can at least create some amazing moments. We all realize that there will be many days that are not amazing. That is factual and expected and a part of life. There is also an old adage to stop and smell the roses. But who literally stops and actually thinks, "I want to create this memory"? The best experience actually comes from using all of your senses at any given moment to create the best memory. You should not only truly take that moment to look at the rose, but you should also smell its fragrance. At that very moment, you should also focus to hear the sounds around you such as the ocean, children laughing, or birds chirping. In addition, what are you feeling? Do you feel the breeze passing over your skin? Of course, using today's technology, you also want to take a picture of special moments, but a picture is only one-dimensional in terms of senses. Do not take excess pictures. In fact, take as few as possible. This moment is about living life and not recording it. In a similar manner, most people don't plan for an amazing day. Don't be most people. Planning is part of the excitement. Find things near where you live that you've never experienced before. Talk to others.

I once read a statement that said something like, "As you get older, you tend to lose your memory, so live unforgettable moments." We should be trying to create those positive, unforgettable moments all our lives. If someone asked you at this moment what was the best about last year, how would you answer? What if they asked whether you were happier last year than any year prior? How would you answer? My advice is that no matter what your answer was to those questions, I wish for you to exceed the number of fabulous times this upcoming year and do things so you are not only happier but much happier. Don't aim for mediocre, aim for outstanding.

The interesting thing about life is that two separate people could experience the exact same day, yet only one sees it as amazing; the other doesn't. Be that person who recognizes more amazing moments and has more amazing days. The reason is clear. There are many around us who aren't happy because of a negative or neutral attitude. There are those you will meet who don't realize how amazing life really is. It all comes down to how each of us think, what we perceive, what we understand, and what we appreciate. That leads to the conclusion that in fact, happiness can be taught or a learned trait. Take for example a very rich man who owns a stunning yacht with which he can cruise the world. Are his amazing days better than mine? Realistically, with such wealth he certainly has the capacity to have a greater number of amazing days because it is amazing what wealth can buy. But even if he can that is not material to me. What is an amazing day? There is no single answer, and it can only be answered truthfully once the day is over. Because as I said before, there are multitudes of people who can live very similar days but at the end of the day do not see it the same way. You can learn to be one of those people who has many more great days and even amazing days than those around you. There are many factors that come into play in any given day. You can greatly control some of the factors, and there are other things that you can't control. As an example, you can control with whom you choose to experience the day. You may have to be quite clear with that individual or those individuals that you want to keep the day intimate and not invite others. Unexpected weather could be a factor, but you can also plan for that. An unforeseen accident or incident may be a factor, but the area you choose to go may reduce such risks. For example, a quiet park has fewer dynamics than last-minute movie tickets. But the most critical factor is you. Only you can create your own happiness, which is a necessary part to creating an amazing day.

What is an amazing day? It's a standout day. It's one of those days where at least a part of it is not forgotten for quite some time, and it is not forgotten only for positive reasons. As an aside, one of my goals is to one day witness two folks who have read this book and are trying to convince the other which one had a more amazing day! I would be immensely proud if I could change two people's lives to such a degree. Does an amazing day require each minute of that day to be amazing to create the amazing day? No, that is way too high a standard. In fact, it would be rare for an amazing day to not have hiccups, but that is part of life and the adventure of living. Thus an amazing day is not something that is critically measured from the moment you wake until you fall asleep. Is a planned amazing day better than a spontaneous amazing day? No. You hope for an amazing day, and when it happens, you enjoy the feeling and the memories. But if you plan an amazing day, and it turns out to be so, as should almost always be the case, you should have the same feeling of happiness and peacefulness. An amazing day is like a perfect day sailing. Just because the wind stopped, causing you to use engines to get home, that doesn't make the day less of an amazing day.

Or perhaps it's like a day in an amusement park with your family, only to discover that your favorite ride is broken down. A positive person and a wise person would never allow such hiccups to ruin a great day. Try to look at things that are perceived in a negative manner in a positive light. Imagine if your favorite ride was not broken down, and you of course chose to ride it. Then while on the ride, it fails. Instead of merely missing the ride, you are stranded on that ride for a couple hours. Now the broken-down ride doesn't seem so bad!

Here is a simple, objective test to know whether you are living life with a positive outlook or manner. Set a timer for two minutes. In that two minutes, write down all the positive experiences you can recall since the beginning of the calendar year. Stop reading for a moment before you proceed. Reset the timer for two minutes and write down all the negative experiences you can recall since the beginning of the calendar year. If you ran out of time when writing down all the positive experiences, you could be a terribly slow writer, or you could be living life in a positive manner. The way to validate this conclusion is to look at your list regarding negative experiences. If the list was nonexistent or short, then you are likely living life in a positive manner because those who live life in a positive manner choose to forget the past negatives unless it is used for a beneficial future lesson (e.g., don't back up into that fire hydrant and cause car damage). If you are recalling negative things like speeding tickets, fights, missing that promotion, or a relationship ending, then you are likely a negative person. The *why* you are living life in a negative manner is not important. The important question is are you ready to change it. If you were a positive person, why would you ever recall most of those negative things? They should essentially be gone from your memory. Thinking of it another way, what is the benefit of recalling those negative things? The goal in life is to live it as happily and positively as you can.

Another way to objectively test whether you're a positive person is to try to spend an entire day specifically thinking of everything in a positive way. It's raining; that's great for the plants. The price of bananas is up; it looks like I'll be buying oranges. That person just ran a red light; thank goodness I was not first to the intersection just as it was turning green. How much effort this takes will tell you objectively whether your outlook is positive or negative. After all, you can't change the price of bananas, make it stop raining, or prevent that other driver from running the red light. Objectively speaking, does recalling a negative thing ever make you feel happier? In contrast, that list of positive things should be exceptionally long. And in fact, the goal of this book is to make it even longer. A great life includes making memories like those great meals you've had, that car ride with the windows down, the smell of fresh grass in the morning, the smell of fresh coffee and bacon at your grandma's, the sound of the waves at the beach, the feeling of the plane door opening to a warm breeze when everyone else is freezing back home, a wedding day, surfing, and watching a child opening gifts at Christmas.

Things that may seem negative may in fact be positive. Are you a person that thinks "I have to" versus "I get to"? There is a huge difference between *I have to* go to work and *I get to* go to work. I *have to* pick up my daughter at school and I *get to* pick up my daughter at school. I *have to* walk the dog and I *get to* walk the dog. Your own mental state and how you view things can completely change your life. Again, don't take things for granted. Even a task such as walking the dog is amazing when you realize how fortunate you are to have your health and to have the ability to care for pet. I can give you a direct example of something that appeared at first to be negative but in fact was quite positive. Ever since I was young, I got headaches. The pain reliever that worked for me was ibuprofen. I kept ibuprofen in my desk at work, in the glove compartment of my vehicles, and at my home. Then one week I was fortunate enough to go on a scuba diving vacation. On that vacation, I helped to move several heavy scuba tanks. What I did not realize at the time is that while moving those tanks in a repetitive manner, I caused my lower back to reach fatigue and then failure. I never felt any pain or discomfort. But when I tried to stand up to get off a plane just twenty-four hours later, I could not move the left side of my body. The injury had caused swelling, which caused a disc in my lower back to rupture. I felt like a stroke victim and needed assistance to get off the plane. I immediately went to see an orthopedic surgeon, who diagnosed my back injury and recommended surgery. I did not elect to have the surgery and chose physical therapy, steroid injections, and acupuncture to heal my back and relieve the pain. At first I could not even bend forward to touch my knees due to the limited movement. For many months, as I was trying different forms of various medical treatments, I experienced pain that seemed to change on a weekly basis from a sensitive left heel to suddenly a sensitive arch on my right foot and various levels of headaches. After those many months of various treatments I misstepped off a curb only to feel an intense pain through my back. I went back to my doctor, who compared my initial MRI to a current MRI, and he told me that nothing had changed. All the treatments, from physical therapy to steroid injections to acupuncture, did not improve the fundamental cause of my pain. My nerve bundle was still being pinched by the shattered disc even with reduced inflammation. With that, I decided to get the back surgery. The incredibly happy ending is that when I woke up from the surgery, it felt like I could run a marathon, and I had no more headaches. It turns out I had a fundamental disk problem that was causing me headaches, but it was not until it actually failed that I became aware of the true cause of my headaches. So what appeared to be bad, when I couldn't even stand up to get off an airplane, turned out to be heaven sent. My headaches are gone, and I feel great. My quality of life increased dramatically. Of course when the injury occurred, I didn't look at it as a positive event, but I also didn't whine about it. I consider myself a positive person, and thus I tried to look at my condition in the most positive light. I had the knowledge that there were other people out there in greater pain than me, and I was fortunate to only have headaches and back pain. I approached it as just another problem that had to be solved. I was seeking the best possible outcome, and thus my first step was to see the best doctor I could find and ask him my options.

Realize that if you have a lot of those amazing days, you will be able to look back and say with strong conviction and confidence that you had an amazing life. Having amazing days is a goal to strive for. That is the high bar standard. When we strive for such a high-bar standard and fall short, it's okay to arrive at great days and great moments. If we fall a little short of that, we have nice days and nice moments. And when we strive for amazing days each of us is going to experience a lot more of those great days and nice days, and that is a great thing. After all this discussion, you must understand that happiness is a perception, an outlook, and an attitude, and it is made up of our senses—the sense of taste, the sense of smell, the sense of sight, the sense of touch, the sense of hearing. But happiness is something we can also learn, just like math or biology. If you own a Ferrari and drive it day after day, that Ferrari can lose its luster, especially if you've never had to drive a clunker. A rich man's child who was perhaps given a Ferrari and was born into that environment will perceive things that you or I consider to be amazing as merely lackluster—and that would be sad. Even if you have earned or been given a lot, it doesn't mean that you can't be wise enough to recognize what you've been given and be thankful for all you receive. And that lesson applies to all of us.

Let's say you receive a gift of tickets to a musical concert. Let's say those tickets are valued at five hundred for the pair. It is a price you simply cannot afford. You are actually trying to put money into a rainy-day fund in preparation of something failing. Maybe you need new tires for your car. Or perhaps you're saving to buy a used car. In any event, those tickets are not affordable to you. Yet you were given them as a gift. You know that the folks who gave you the tickets are very well off. To them, the five hundred dollars is minor in their household budget. How thankful should you be for the gift? Is it sufficient to send a thank-you text? Is a thank-you email sufficient? The answer is emphatically no to both of those questions. The standard is not what they can afford. In this instance, the standard is what you can afford. And you cannot afford the five-hundred-dollar concert tickets. Hence that is an incredible gift to you. Thus, the very least you should do is take the time to send a thank-you note in writing. Or perhaps do something special as a thank-you for the gift, such as help in some capacity with something they need.

Let's change the scenario a little bit and say that the people who gave you the tickets were friends who could not afford them either. They were given the tickets by someone else but could not attend the concert themselves. Does that mean you should value them more? No. Again, the standard is not what someone who gave you the gift can afford but what you can afford. You need to send your friend that same thank-you note in writing or do something special for the gift given you. Let's change the scenario one further time and say that you can afford the five-hundred-dollar tickets but chose not to buy them. Now a friend offers you a pair of tickets to go with them. In that instance, the most valued response is something personal from you once again. It is still not an email or a text. Email and text are low standards. They take no effort and generally don't convey sincerity. People who care about each other should be replying with sincerity in whatever measure that means. If they are close friends, it may mean a firm hug. Perhaps it is dinner out together. Perhaps it is dinner and a movie. You should treat them as you would want to be treated if you had given them such a gift.

By simply asking yourself what is or is not amazing about your day, you will begin to learn what are parts of an amazing day, as well as those things that are not part of what you'd identify as an amazing day. For example, I know of no one who would begin to create an amazing day itinerary which included foods they dislike, people they dislike, bad weather (unless an amazing day is being a storm chaser), or paying bills. Most people might think an amazing day scenario is like the planning of a wedding day, and a wedding day is a good test case to follow. Can a wedding day be an amazing day? The answer is most certainly yes. But it is amazing how many brides and grooms are disappointed with the actual wedding day, and that is a true shame. The wedding day is a unique day where it is common for a lot of folks to be involved to witness the ceremony. Thus, a lot of things have to converge at the right time for things to be perfect.

Instead of the wedding couple looking for an amazing day they look to a higher standard of having a perfect day. What a wedding couple should be told in advance and fully understand is that there are too many factors or variables involved to make a wedding day perfect. But it certainly could and should be an amazing day. What do I mean by a perfect day? That is a higher standard than an amazing day. A perfect day is where not only does everything that is planned go as planned, but also it exceeds your expectations. So the birth of a child is almost always a perfect day, and I find it is rare for me to meet a parent of a healthy newborn who doesn't say the day was perfect. That is because the birth of their child is so beyond emotion that all the other factors disappear around the event. And that is how a wedding day should be. If the wedding couple were merely focused on each other instead of all the ancillary happenings, then the day would turn out perfect. It is not uncommon on a wedding day to have the band cancel at the last minute. That is why you need a backup in the plan. You have to realize that not all of the guests will like the food. Maybe someone will be sick on the wedding day, or perhaps the power goes out. With all those things going wrong, can it still be a perfect day? The answer is a resounding yes, just as the birth of a child during a lightning storm when the power goes out is still a perfect day. But if you are truly bothered by things going wrong, then the lesson of creating an amazing day is to keep it simple. In general, you shouldn't have it involve too many people unless it is a team event you are planning, like a skydiving formation or a large sporting event. But the true fact is you shouldn't be bothered by things going wrong; if you are, you definitely need to keep reading this book!

When planning an amazing day, try to keep it simple with a limited number of activities. For example, it is easier to plan an amazing day with a picnic than at a restaurant because you limit the variables. What if the restaurant lost your reservation? What if the food comes out poorly? What if your car is damaged in the parking lot? In the same regard, imagine you're trying to plan an amazing vacation that lasts one week. Generally speaking, you want to avoid as much as possible things on that vacation that aren't enjoyable. As an example, you would not want to spend most of the seven days driving in your car or riding on a bus and trying to get to four different locations. Given the planning option, it would be wiser to stay in one location for seven days.

One of my amazing days was with my dad. His memory was diminishing because of a stroke he had experienced. They tell you that you'll lose your mind when you grow older. What they don't tell you is that you won't miss it very much. While on a beach vacation, I was able to take him to the Disney animated movie *Up*, which he thoroughly enjoyed. We followed that movie with bowling and then went to a great meal, where he enjoyed a cold beer. He was smiling all day and even reached out to hug me and tell me that he was proud of me. It was indeed an amazing day. Even though it was an incredibly simple day, it is one I will never forget. My father has since passed, and even though we met several people on that day, not one of them could have realized the joy I was feeling. In fact, even my dad could not realize how lucky I felt that day due to his condition. I have been fortunate to have some fabulous days that I will always remember. That is one of them.

Another suggestion to have an amazing day is to plan for it each year. Perhaps it's your half birthday, meaning the annual date midway between your birthdays. If you can't have an amazing day, then plan an amazing hour—and have that hour five days in a row. That does not mean that you sit in front of a television. It means you do something special during that hour that you normally would not do. Try to find things that you're passionate about and include as many of those into your amazing day. Create an elaborate surprise for someone that begins with a scavenger hunt. Alternatively, write a love poem for a special someone and have the airline cabin staff read it over the loudspeaker: "For my stunningly beautiful, amazingly generous, insanely kind wife in 24C; I choose us." Or be even more erotic and write a love poem on your lover where it cannot be seen by others. If you have a close family or close group of friends, you can create the tradition of a pledge getaway. The pledge getaway can be once a year or even once every five years. You all pledge to meet and do something together. It may be a pledge to meet at a spa, go camping, go on a cruise, or go on a bike ride. Perhaps the pledge includes doing something unique each time you meet. Perhaps a hot air balloon ride, snow skiing, scuba diving, baking class, wine tasting, or an amazing picnic in a different national park each time you meet. Make the experience memorable as a group. You will find happiness in not just the getaway but in the fun in planning the getaway as a group.

Do you love to scuba dive, read, take hot air balloon rides, take family picnics, ride a Harley, bird watch, white water raft, fish with your dad, or ice skate with your mom? The perfect formula is combining things you love with people whom you love. Think of providing others the amazing day. I remember an amazing day for me was Christmas morning when my daughters were young. They were so excited to see what Santa brought them and placed under the tree. Try to create an amazing day model. Look back on your life and write down amazing days. What about those days were amazing? How can you best recreate part or all of those experiences. Can you create that experience for someone else? One suggestion for providing that amazing day is to get out any saved holiday cards (everything from Mother's Day to Valentine's Day), anniversary cards, or written notes and have a picnic with the person who gave you those cards or notes. Read them again together. The experience of reliving great days and great times will reconnect you with that special person with renewed memories and fondness. It's sad to know that the pictures you take are really special to only you and your immediate loved ones. Even the differences between generations make the interest diminish with minor exceptions. Grandchildren are not really interested in pictures of the one-room schoolhouse. But that is how it's supposed to be. Children are supposed to grow up, and if the parents have done well, then they also grow out of being children and become their own adults with their own interests. The hope is that they have also found a passion in life. Perhaps it's scuba diving, perhaps it's flying a plane, perhaps it's cooking that amazing cupcake, perhaps it's nursing a sick animal, or perhaps it's solving a complex math problem.

The best day of your life most likely will not be one that you created to experience an amazing day, and that is a good thing, although clearly an incredibly wonderful day could readily arise out of an amazing day plan. In fact, that is my wish. It would be wonderful for that to happen repeatedly. An amazing day is something that you can plan for or be open to and happen all on its own. An incredibly wonderful day is something that simply happens. The stars align. You plan a picnic on a mountain, and you witness a rainbow just as your partner is telling you for the first time that he is falling in love with you. The walk up the mountain is along a stream that is normally a dry basin. The trip back down presents an amazing sunset. And for dinner, you are seated at a table overlooking the valley and can see for miles. When you have these incredibly wonderful days, I always suggest at the end of the evening to sit down, pull out a journal, and write down everything you can recall of that day—the scent of the forest, where you parked the car, what car you were driving, the songs you heard, the location of where you first held hands, who was your waiter, what did you order. You will never regret having such memories written down. Especially if you are recording those memories with someone incredibly special. You'll be able to share them together perhaps ten or fifteen years later. All positive. All exciting. All recorded based on all five of your senses. What did you taste, touch, hear, see, and smell? Taking the lessons of this chapter, you should recognize that the less you take for granted and the more you focus on positive things in your life, the more you will begin to live a happier life.

Think backward to great days you've had in your life. Then analyze them and determine what made them great. Is there a common thread? I would suspect that a common theme may be the fact that you shared that experience with someone else. That is not to say that a great day could not be lying on a hammock and finishing that great book uninterrupted. But an amazing day should be one that you could repeat for the rest of your life, and each day you go to bed still think it was an amazing day. When you first try planning an amazing day, you may wish to start by trying to pick someone that you feel would truly appreciate some experience or gift that you could provide. Thus, if you live in a neighborhood where kids are spoiled to a high degree, then it is unlikely one of those kids would truly appreciate a gift such as a trip to an amusement park with your family. It is unfortunate that in our society, few children and even adults deeply appreciate not only what they are given but also what they earn. I grew up with little, although it was a safe neighborhood. I worked to buy clothes that I wanted to wear because my mom would spend only a limited amount on each child for school clothes. I delivered newspapers, mowed lawns, and did other odd jobs to earn money until I had enough to buy what I needed. My first job with a paycheck was as a dishwasher at a restaurant. I had to borrow my dad's car and always had to put fuel back in it when I did. Because I grew up with little, I am very thankful, even today, when I am treated to something no matter how small. And I am especially thankful if the gift came from someone with little.

Chapter Six

How to Reduce the Number of Rough Pebbles in Your Life and Other Odds and Ends

COULD YOU HAVE AN AMAZING day the day after you get fired? Absolutely. Getting fired might turn out to be the best thing that ever happened to you. I began the previous chapter with objective tools to help create amazing days. On the other side of the coin are tools to help you prevent negative interactions so your day and life are happier. These are lifelong tools. Let me state at the outset that like most children, I got yelled at if I did something wrong, or at least if someone else thought what I was doing was wrong. Perhaps I was yelled at because I didn't put out the garbage. Perhaps I left lights on. Perhaps I didn't shut the refrigerator door or the front door of the house. Perhaps I accidentally scratched my dad's car. Perhaps my parents got a call from the school for something I allegedly did. In each of those instances, I was being conditioned to respond to this yelling (or worse) with a positive action. As a result, I turned the lights off. I made sure the refrigerator door or front door was closed. That said, after I left the house as an adult and began to make my own decisions, I quickly decided I am not going to reward others for treating me poorly. I also recognized, very objectively, that I continue to see the lesson of awarding or condoning poor behavior in all forms of our media and even in our entertainment.

Let me make something truly clear. I never reward negative behavior. I will repeat that because of its importance to me: I never reward negative behavior. So what do I do when someone acts negatively toward me? I will tell you a system that I have followed now for many years. When I was in my late twenties, I recognized a fact that seems acceptable in society but not to me. I see numerous instances where negative behavior is tolerated, accepted, or even rewarded. When I am confronted with rude behavior or a similar negative action, I "disarm" the person by putting out my hand and saying, "Hello, my name is Dave. I'm sorry, what is yours?" That simple action, statement, and question almost always forces a reasonable person to stop and consider answering my question. When they do, I ask a follow-up question. Let me give you a true example of an experience I had with a prior neighbor. This was my first encounter with the neighbor, who lived directly behind me and whom I had never met.

The backyard of my property had a chain-link fence. I was replacing it with a six-foot-tall privacy fence made of cedar. It was a beautiful cedar privacy fence. I hired a company and instructed the two workers on the exact scope of the work. The first step was to remove the chain-link fence because the replacement fence material was on site and ready to be installed. I had reached out to my rear yard neighbors as a courtesy, just in case they had pets, to tell them of my new fence. One particular neighbor was never home when I visited their house. As the workers began to remove the chain-link fence, that rear neighbor ran from his home to our shared property line and started yelling at the workers and asking them what they were doing. I was inside the house at the time but my amazingly wonderful wife saw or heard the commotion and called for my help. I walked to the back of the property where the workers were located and stopped at the chain link fence line. The neighbor was still yelling at my workers. He was one of the "rough pebbles" that you cannot avoid in your life and that you need to deal with directly.

I did not respond to what my neighbor was saying because he was clearly being negative. I also realized that starting a yelling match never accomplishes anything; in fact it usually escalates the situation. So as always, I was patient and eventually made eye contact with my rear neighbor. I interrupted his diatribe by putting out my hand and saying my usual words. "Hello, my name is Dave. I'm sorry, what is yours?" He hesitated for quite a few moments and then told me his name. I always find it interesting how a personal question as simple as your name disarms a person to some degree. I think most folks feel intimidated or think they lose some control when they have to give out their name. I'll call my neighbor Mike for this story. I said, "Well, good morning, Mike. How can I help you?" Mike was concerned about the fence and started to raise his voice again. I raised my hand in a stop signal motion that he could clearly see. As he paused, I said very calmly and clearly, "Mike, we have just met. But I will tell you that I do not reward negative behavior. If you choose to raise your voice instead of having a polite discussion, then we have nothing to talk about." He was dumbfounded, which I find is a common result of my system. Again, the raising of my hand in a stop motion instead of raising my voice almost always gets the same reaction. I suppose the person is dumbfounded with the hand motion because they are not used to someone ignoring their bombastic speech. I asked him if he wanted to start over again before I left and my workers proceeded with their work. He then told me that he wasn't asked about the fence. I told him that the fence was totally on my property by a matter of inches, and hence he had no say regarding my property. I told him I had the site survey that legally proved my claim. I told him that I would be a polite neighbor and leave up the chain-link fence if he so desired, but if I did, I was erecting the privacy fence tight against it to maximize my yard size. Thus from his vantage point, he would see the chain-link fence abutted against the beautiful privacy fence. The chain-link fence would be hidden from me, which was all I wanted as an outcome. I also told him politely that I would not give him future permission to remove the chain-link fence because I did not want the new privacy fence damaged.

I told Mike he had to make an immediate decision because my workers had to begin with the work. Did he desire to see a chain-link fence up against the cedar privacy fence, or did he want a clear view of a beautiful cedar fence? As expected, he chose to have the chain-link fence removed. I told Mike it was a sincere pleasure meeting him and that I wished our first meeting had not been over a misunderstanding. I then went back into the house. I never had a problem with Mike again. Now, you may ask, "What does this have to do with happiness in one's life?" This example will help you to recognize negative behavior and hopefully stop others from being negative toward you. In fact, I hope Mike learned something and will not be rude to others in the future. You will find that your day can be much happier if you stop rewarding people who are negative toward you; that includes family, friends, and acquaintances. And if each of us can teach at least two people that we will not reward negative behavior think how nice our society could become.

Another strategy to disarm people who are clearly upset is to ask them in a calm manner why they are so unhappy. This can be disarming to folks. Tell them that if they were a very happy person, they wouldn't be upset, and thus something else must really be bothering them. Tell them that you're willing to listen to what is truly bothering them. Say that you can help. But tell them that means they have to stop yelling. Set some ground rules to begin the conversation, such as the need to sit down and close their eyes for thirty seconds without speaking. It is very hard to remain angry when seated with your hands on your lap and your eyes closed.

Never reward someone yelling at you or others. This also means you do not ignore hate. I find it disgusting to see video where someone is being hurt, and there are bystanders, who greatly outnumber the perpetrator, watching and not willing to help. What if the person being harmed was your grandfather, mother, brother, or daughter? Would you stand by and watch? The time is always right to do the right thing. That person is someone's mother, brother, or daughter. Act. Now, this does not mean to act if your personal safety is clearly in danger because you are greatly outnumbered. This does not mean to act if someone has an overwhelming weapon. But getting your butt kicked when trying to help someone else is a very reasonable price to pay if you can help. Otherwise, offer as much assistance as you can as quickly as you can.

I find that when people are agitated or yelling, visual cues like putting forward a kind hand works to interrupt that yelling. When people are yelling, they are not listening, so they cannot hear or comprehend what you are saying. Yelling back solves nothing. Be patient. Raise a hand like a stop sign, or put out a hand for a handshake. Everybody understands those hand gestures. Another way in some situations is to ask, "Bob, do you reward people who yell at you by doing what they want? I certainly do not. So you need to be polite and respectful if you want me to listen." By the way, if you follow this method, make sure the guy's name is Bob! Do not be a friend to anyone who exhibits hate or negative judgment. Get away from those type of people. They are the opposite of adding happiness to your life. Be honest when evaluating other people's character and trust your instincts. There are thousands of people around us who are kind. Seek them out. Imagine a world without hate. Do not reward a single person who hates, and certainly not with your friendship or trust.

To show you how commonplace negative behavior is, let me give you two quick examples with which you are likely familiar. The first is an extremely popular movie, *Shrek*. At least part of the targeted audience for this movie was children and young adults. However, there are many humorous elements in the movie that specifically pertain to adults. In the movie, an ogre, Shrek, rescues Princess Fiona. During the rescue, Shrek is wearing a helmet. After the actual rescue, Fiona wants to see what Shrek looks like. In the movie, she first says in a somewhat nice voice, "Now, remove your helmet."

Shrek replies also in a nice voice, "Look, I really don't think this is a good idea."

Fiona replies in an agitated voice, "Just take off the helmet."

Shrek replies, still in a nice voice, "I'm not going to."

Fiona is now clearly agitated and says, "Take it off." Shrek says no. Fiona now yells at him and says "Now!"

Shrek says, "Okay, easy. As you command, Your Highness." He rewards her for yelling at him by doing what she wants and removes his helmet. This is a family movie, and this scene never got any attention that I am aware of. And once again, it is teaching the target audience, children, to reward negative behavior.

The second example is a commercial that was repeatedly aired just recently. Because it was repeatedly aired, it would seem the advertisers believed it would promote their product. I found it taught the wrong lesson of rewarding negative behavior, and thus I would not be interested in purchasing a product that promotes such ideas. The commercial is an insurance commercial. In the commercial, there is a married man on a late-night phone call to his insurance agent. The commercial is supposed to show that you can call at any hour of the day or night to get service. The man in the commercial is heard telling the agent, "Yeah, I'm married. Does that matter? You can do that for me, really? I'd like that."

Suddenly a light turns on, and there is the man's wife, who enters the room and asks in a demanding and negative voice to her husband, "Who are you talking to?" The husband politely and immediately responds to her question and identifies whom he is talking to. That is the first instance that the husband rewards his wife for being mean to him. The wife then literally grabs the phone from her husband and speaks into the phone, asking, "Who is this?" Now the wife has effectively called her husband a liar because he already answered her question of who was on the phone. He politely and kindly answered her question. That is the second instance that the husband rewards his wife for being mean to him, by not objecting to the question or showing any signs of being disappointed or upset. The wife then says in a nasty demeanor, "She sounds hideous."

The husband responds with, "Well, she's a guy, so ..." That is the third time the wife is mean to her husband. This commercial is teaching the audience, or perhaps women, not to trust their husbands. It teaches men to reward woman who yell at them, and effectively call them a liar, with kindness. It appears so commonplace in households that commercials are made to model those relationships. Yet I failed to see any outcry about this commercial. If the fictitious man was just dating that woman, instead of being married to her, would he have asked her on a second date? If this was an example of a marriage, how long do you think that marriage would last? Do you think either of those partners would be genuinely happy in that marriage? My very first critical factor in a marriage is your absolute ability to fully trust them as you would your (model) parent. Was that exhibited in the commercial? And when I say truly happy, I mean that feeling of excitement each time you see each other, and that feeling of something deeply missing when you're apart. Do you think this fictitious wife would deeply miss her husband during the day when they were apart? Why didn't the insurance company run a follow-up commercial where the wife apologizes for her actions and adds a twist to the commercial that still promotes the politeness and trustworthiness of the insurance company? It's likely because they didn't even understand the issues that are taught in the commercial. I certainly didn't find it humorous. And if the intent was one of humor, is that the best commercial they could have run? Does that commercial best represent their product? A second follow-up commercial could have been a win-win. There are endless examples I could provide you in this book about negative behavior being rewarded, but they would all be repeats of these two similar examples. Simply turn on a "reality" show, and within the first several minutes, you'll likely witness yelling or negative behavior. It is terrible that so many of us have become blind to its presence because it is so omnipresent. Why it is that any riot could become justifiable? I certainly hope you realize that reality shows are not reality; they are staged or scripted like all other programming. Ask yourself, "Am I happier because I watch such shows?" Is your time valuable to you? Is your time better spent in some other manner? How about spending that same time learning something new, going on a walk, calling relatives, or planning an amazing day?

When you are confronted with negative behavior, I hope you do not reward it. This rule affects everyone you interact with, and it absolutely includes disrespectful children and all family members. Also, do not reward a nasty partner. You can ask very polite and simple questions such as, "Do you truly believe that yelling at me makes me love you more? Is this the way you promised to make my day better? Is this making me want to date you again tomorrow? If a stranger was watching us would they think we were very much in love? Do you feel happier yelling at me? Am I the most important person in your life? Would you treat your mom as you just treated me?" It also applies to everyday acquaintances and situations. This system lets the rude person know that the behavior is not acceptable to you. Hopefully the rude person will also not be rude to someone else if they understand the lesson. If we all practiced not rewarding negative behavior, the result would be a lot more kindness. The interesting outcome is that the rude person may change their behavior because it's actually exhausting being mean, and I mean that objectively. Try to be mean for an entire day versus practicing kindness all day. It's exhausting to be angry for any long period of time. Yet one could be happy for an endless period of time with boundless energy.

I fully encourage you to follow my system: put out your hand and introduce yourself first and then ask for their name. People intuitively don't like to provide a stranger with anything personal, so giving out their true name can be somewhat disarming to a frustrated person. You might notice a hesitation when they slowly provide you their name and wonder what is going on. Then say, "I understand we have just met. But I will tell you that I do not reward negative behavior. If you choose to raise your voice instead of having a polite discussion, then we have nothing to talk about," or something similar. You can develop your own system that you are comfortable with to make your day happier. I have also stepped in when I witnessed someone being rude. I was in line at a coffee shop where a rude younger customer said their coffee was not hot enough in an agitated way, instead of using politeness. I stepped beside the rude customer, extended my hand in a kind gesture to the coffee shop worker, and said, "I'm sorry. I believe this young man is just in a hurry. What he meant to politely ask was, Would you please make his coffee extra hot? He'd greatly appreciate it." The rude customer stood dumbfounded as I took the coffee cup from him and handed it to the worker. I said, "Thank you," and stepped back in line. The rude person clearly learned a lesson. I didn't have to say anything else. This is just one of many examples I have experienced in my life.

Another thing I've learned in life to make life easier is to adopt systems for tasks that you perform repeatedly. A repeatable system makes life easier. I have a system for where the car keys go. I have a system for how to pack a suitcase so nothing is left behind. I even have a system to mark the outside of all my suitcases when I travel so they are readily identifiable at the airport. I have a system for making sure I have my wallet and cell phone as I walk out the door. What is my system? I put my wallet and cell phone with my car keys because I know I am taking the car. It is simple and repeatable. Those are the best kind of systems. I have a system for how my cell phone is charged.

I have noted the positive aspects of creating lists for critical elements. That said, you have to balance when a list is necessary or beneficial versus creating a system. The simple standard is to establish a system when it makes life easier. A simple example is a system for household necessities. Let's take the specific example of toilet paper. You should have a system in place on where the toilet paper is specifically stored. It should be stored in a specific closet on a specific shelf so that the storage location doubles as a notification of when a new purchase is necessary. Let's say you buy toilet paper in bulk of twenty-four rolls, and let's say your home has three bathrooms. You begin by placing three rolls in each bathroom. If supply goes low in an individual bathroom, you'll go to that main closet supply location to resupply. When the main supply goes low, you know it is time to repurchase your twenty-four rolls. This system is simple, and it works even if you have a lot of visitors and the demand goes up. The main supply location will provide you the notice. Before you go shopping, you need only stop by the closet and see whether a purchase is necessary. A simple system can help you to create an efficient shopping list.

For example, a shopping list can be added to throughout the week if you shop on weekends. You keep the shopping list in one location so it is easily located and edited. But there is also a system for actually taking the shopping list with you before you leave the house to perform the actual shopping. My simple system to remember the actual shopping list is to place the list, after I've completed it, with my car keys. This is a simple system because I know I must have my car keys to start the car. That's a simple and flawless system. These systems are not truly about adding happiness but about avoiding frustration. They make life easier, and that makes me happier. Systems also make you more efficient. Don't hesitate to be a systems person.

Other rough pebbles in life are things like temptation, risky behavior, peer pressure, and envy. None of these will result in a happier life, much less a happier experience. Does an incredibly happy person even think of temptation or envy, much less act on it? If you're thoroughly enjoying playing tennis with three friends, does the thought of stealing enter your mind? Do you envy what type of car someone drove to the match? Of course not; you are very happy playing the game you enjoy. If you are very happy while on a date with your partner, are you thinking of breaking into the cash register or stealing a designer purse? No way. Thus, something is already lacking in your life if you have envy or temptation.

Let's first talk about temptation. By definition, it is the desire to do something, especially something wrong or unwise. Envy, by definition, is a feeling of discontented or resentful longing aroused by someone else's possessions, qualities, or luck. Examples of temptation are stealing those sneakers from the store or eating those six donuts when you're on a diet. Examples of envy are wishing you were as popular as someone else or desiring the car your neighbor has. Notice that I did not state simply desiring a nice car that is common to a lot of folks and is not unhealthy. No one wants a car that is undependable or rusting. There is huge difference between need and envy. You need a roof over your head to protect yourself from the weather and bugs. That is totally different from envying someone who has a luxury home on twenty acres and horses.

Peer pressure is normally thought of as an experience of youth, but there are a lot of adults who do things only because an acquaintance or so-called friend urges them to do so. There are also a lot of adults who want to keep up with the Joneses. Risky behavior can happen at any age. Just like temptation and envy, peer pressure and risky behavior are not something that is of interest to someone who is extremely happy. The extremely happy person is not looking for something more because there is no need for something more. A person who understands the critical elements of happiness is thankful for what they have and what they are given. If you understand and learn this, then you have already gone a long way toward a happier life. There is no benefit to you to think that the grass is greener on the other side of the fence. Just because someone has a nicer car, nicer house, or more money, that does not mean they are happier than you. And even if they were happier than you, it is not their fault. It is yours. If you understand this book, you should understand that you can learn to be happy by first appreciating what you have. You should understand that jealousy will poison you, and hate will destroy you. What difference does it make to a child if they play in the mud or play in a pool? It doesn't because they have not learned envy or jealousy. They are all false idols that do not benefit you and definitely will not make you suddenly happier. Those are not the things in life that can bring happiness. When you are old and gray, you will likely have fonder memories of when you sat on a porch as a kid, drank lemonade, and chatted with your friends than any time you checked your social media on your phone as an adult.

The worst of these four rough pebbles is risky behavior. It is risky behavior that can result in the loss of your life or the most harm. Yet those who take those risks likely never understand or contemplate the true worst-case scenario. There are endless examples of risky behavior that could be life-changing or life-ending. People lose their lives every year from walking out on ice, flying an aircraft into poor weather conditions, driving a car in bad weather, driving a car with worn brakes, driving and using a cell phone, walking into a crosswalk of a busy road while focused on their phones, accelerating at an extremely high rate of speed, going for a hike without sufficient supplies, riding a bike too fast, trying a street drug, doing something illegal, abusing a legal drug, and so on. So the question is, How do we avoid these rough pebbles?

The answer is objectively quite simple: knowledge. Knowledge that the risk you are about to take is not worth it. Knowledge that those who are trying to force or encourage you to do something that you don't want to do are not your friends. Knowledge that any such risk will not make you happier even if you succeed. You should stay away from anyone who encourages such behavior. Do not trust them with any aspect of your life. Ask an objective question: "Exactly how is this person making my life happier or more fulfilling and helping me stay true to my core principles and reach my goals?" Another way to determine whether something is the right thing to do is to substitute the action with someone you respect. "What would my grandfather say or what would my mom say if they found out I was doing this?" Also follow your instincts. Do not get into that car if you do not believe the driver will protect you. Do not get into that aircraft if you do not trust the condition of the aircraft or the environment. In terms of envy, if you understand the critical elements of happiness, why would you care about what other people think about your house or car? Why do you need a house or car like theirs when your home or car suits all your needs?

Another rough pebble is your own self-worth or ego. How do you avoid having a grandiose ego? The solution is simple. Never feel as though you are the most important person in any room. Always treat others as you would want to be treated. Don't assume you are seated at the head of the table. Thus when you are asked to take the seat at the head of the table, you will feel delighted.

A lack of confidence can be another rough pebble. If in the past, you hesitated from doing something because you were nervous, change that behavior. Just ask. The answer might still be no, but that is okay because that was the answer if you never asked. Again, just ask. What's the worst that could happen? There are a lot of books on objective things you can do to gain confidence, but a common thread is knowledge.

There is a saying that what is truly most valuable is often underrated by most. That is true for those who do not genuinely appreciate each experience. When you have children, it is all about time. It is not about quality as much as it is about quantity, if possible. The time you spend with your children, such as spending the night in a tent in the backyard, will be lifelong memories for you and them. Seek those moments. Cram as many of those into your lifetime as you can. A simple backyard tent sleepover may be underrated for most but not for those who understand what the entire experience means to your children. It won't matter that it rains during the night and your family dog, soaking wet, runs into the tent and immediately shakes off the water spraying everyone. Actually, it does matter when you react with laughing and guffawing versus being upset and yelling. It might even be a lifetime gleeful moment that was just created.

Chapter Seven
Some Objective Strengths You'll Need for a Happier Life

ANOTHER CRITICAL PART OF HAPPINESS is for you to objectively decide what type of life you want to lead. Your happiness is totally up to you. I submit that the path you choose will cause you to make specific choices. Those choices will include everything from the people you choose to have around you to the programs you choose to watch and even the area you choose to live in. When you were a child and your parent told you to "go be happy for two hours" you'd likely run out the front door and go find a friend. Maybe you'd go bike riding or go swim in a pond. Now as an adult if someone told you to "go be happy for two hours" you might go to a wine bar with a friend or start an art project or get a spa treatment. What if as an adult someone told you to "go be happy for ten years" how would you do that? It is a fact that what makes each of us happy will change in our own lifetimes. Therefor it is not a surprise to understand that it is also true that what makes each one of us, as a unique individual, happy will also be different. Thus I cannot produce a list of what makes people happy. Being happy is more about you as an individual, how you think, your attitude, the choices you make. It is directly affected by both your experiences and your knowledge. Even two children that had very similar experiences by being raised in the same family will not find happiness in the identical way. But what is important is that there are some common threads that we all need to be happy. This book analyzes those common threads. Can we model an amazing life? No, that is not realistic because a life is not made up of just "go be happy for two hours". You can't just keep repeating those "two hours" over and over and result in a happy life. Life is "go be happy for 80 years". This is a book to teach you how to be happy for 80 years and more. To make my initial point, I'd like to quote a very meaningful proverb to me.

> An old Cherokee is teaching his grandson about life. "A fight is going on inside me," he said to the boy. "It is a terrible fight, and it is between two wolves. One is evil—he is anger, envy, sorrow, regret, greed, arrogance, self-pity, guilt, resentment, inferiority, lies, false pride, superiority, and ego." He continued, "The other is good—he is joy, peace, love, hope, serenity, humility, kindness, benevolence, empathy, generosity, truth, compassion, and faith. The same fight is going on inside you—and inside every other person, too.
>
> The grandson thought about it for a minute and then asked his grandfather, "Which wolf will win?"
>
> The old Cherokee simply replied, "The one you feed."

This proverb is very meaningful to me for the words chosen associated with bad/evil and those chosen to describe good. But I also find the proverb interesting in that the question isn't which one will die but instead which one will win. To me, that means we can choose elements of evil at any time because it remains inside us. Evil may be within us in a very weakened state, but it is not totally dead. I also found the term *feed* meaningful. Most of us understand the term *feed* to mean something that is both necessary and a reasonably constant need for us to survive, meaning that we have no choice but to face this decision between evil and good on a reasonably constant basis. What this proverb doesn't tell you is that choosing the exclusive path of good is a much easier path. This proverb also does not address a third option wherein people choose neither side. Hopefully, no one reading this book would be the person who chooses not to act at all. The reason I say that choosing the path of good is an easier path is because choosing to be angry all the time is exhausting, and you feel agitated or unrested the whole time you're in that state. That is also true about envy and the other terms associated with evil. How terrible a life it would be if you chose to be envious of everyone, or of anyone! Again, this is the opposite of seeking happiness. I assure you that I can readily look around and find men younger than me, smarter than me, more attractive than me, richer than me, and stronger than me. But what is the benefit of even thinking about those traits relative to oneself? Nothing. Because none of that matters; it is simply noise to ignore.

What lies behind us and what lies before us are small matters compared to what lies within us. I would like to pose a simple example. Let's say that you were driving in your car with a friend. You were both enjoying an enlightened conversation, and you unknowingly pass the exit you were supposed to take. You now have to drive over a full mile, with several traffic lights, and double back to get back to that exit location. There is a large majority of people who get terribly upset or frustrated when they miss their turn. There are those who will immediately blame someone else in the car, and an argument ensues. But a person who understands the critical elements of happiness does not do so. A person with an understanding of the critical elements looks at things quite differently even when given the same set of facts. A person with understanding considers the what-ifs and analyzes the pros and cons and realizes you can't change the past. A person with understanding quickly concludes that it is a fact that the exit was missed. Now the next question is, How it is best remedied? What is the benefit of being upset due to the missed turn? I will tell you with absolute clarity that there is none. After all, this is going to happen again in life. You will miss turns. You can create a system to miss less turns, like maybe increase the voice volume on a GPS system, but you're still going to miss a turn or two, especially if you don't have a GPS system or it fails. You can establish a system that when you are coming up to a turn, you focus on the task at hand and avoid conversation not relevant to the task. In fact, this is a rule for airline pilots when they are about to land. They are not allowed to have small talk in the cockpit for obvious reasons: it is a time of high workload for a pilot. A person with the understanding of the critical elements of happiness will objectively ask whether being upset due to the missed turn makes him a safer driver because he has not yet gotten to his destination. Would he now be more alert, or would he be frustrated and make spur-of-the-moment decisions that are possibly dangerous? A person with understanding acknowledges that a person who is upset is more likely to speed or run a yellow light in an effort to maintain some artificial timeline to the destination.

Now, what if I give you a little more information and tell you that when our driver was passing that exit, he also noticed a yellow sedan behind him who happened to take the exact exit? When our driver finally gets back to that same exit ramp that he missed, he gets down to the bottom of the ramp, where there is an intersection and traffic light. At that intersection, he sees that same yellow sedan, which was just behind him but took the exit, hit in the front end by a motorist who ran a red light. If our driver had taken the exit just ahead of the yellow sedan, there is a high likelihood, based on the close spacing between him and the yellow sedan, that it would have been him in that accident. A person with an understanding of the critical elements of happiness does not get frustrated or upset when they miss an exit ramp. They understand that there is not only no benefit to being frustrated but that it could also be harmful. They merely understand it to be a fact. But it is also in the past. They may even think of what they may have avoided. Maybe they would have avoided that accident. Maybe because they were delayed, they got a better hotel room. Their delay caused them to arrive at the front desk of the hotel just as a stunning suite was fully cleaned and available. The point is you'll never know. But you do know that focusing on the negative is not a benefit. Thus a critical element is to not focus on the negative. A person with the understanding tries to eliminate the negative as quickly as possible. Negativity comes in many forms. It comes in the form of worry, envy, jealousy, sadness, frustration, and hate, to name a few. A person with an understanding of the critical elements of happiness can objectively understand the true and objective benefit of something as simple as sitting on a couch and thinking of joyful things versus focusing on hate. Hate harms others temporarily, but it harms you forever if that is your inner self. The latter is very destructive to your own health and mental state. Even though this person is sitting on the same couch, the difference is extreme in terms of quality of life merely because of the way they think. That is the power of thought. You must choose happiness. With everything I discuss in this book, it is still up to you. You will be as happy as you make up your mind to be.

Is your day better if you waste time thinking of how to get revenge on the person who put a ding in your car door or is it better being focused on making that colleague laugh when you tell him about some embarrassing moment you had? A person without understanding is the person who remains frustrated and likely speeds because they missed the exit, resulting in another accident. A person who understands the critical elements of happiness also understands that failure and mistakes are a part of life. If you are an engineer designing a device, you produce that device first and actually make various tests to find out its greatest weakness. Then you design to overcome that weakness to make the device that much better. Infants don't simply get up and run; they fall many times and learn from their mistakes to gain balance. A person who understands the critical elements of happiness is always looking for balance and looks at failure not as a negative but as a part of life. Failure is merely an unplanned outcome. In fact, failure has led to many great discoveries such as penicillin, Teflon, and the microwave. Thus a person with the understanding doesn't look at failure as a negative but more like an opportunity. She looks at something where others have failed as a likely place for opportunity and success.

The proverb and example hopefully helped you to objectively understand a mental part to happiness. As I noted in chapter one, only you can make yourself happy. Choosing to be happy is a constant decision-making process, and that is a good thing. You will need to make decisions literally every day, if not every hour or minute, that will keep you on a course to living a happy life. When you're about to make one of those decisions, do not aim for simply happy but aim for happiest. Why choose to use ordinary dinnerware when your favorite silver is sitting on a shelf? Which one makes you happier? Why choose to stay at home when a friend has invited you bowling? There are also environmental factors that will affect you, how you feel about your work, the amount of physical exercise you participate in, the food that you eat, the area that you live in, and possibly how the weather is in that area. These will all be addressed later in this book. For example, I know for a fact that I feel more fatigue when I experience multiple days of rain or overcast in a row. It is an objective fact that I understand about my body. I feel less driven, less motivated, unless I get in direct sunlight within a reasonable period of time. Thus where I choose to live is a critical element to me. But understand that these are all critical factors when your goal is to live the happiest life you possibly can. We are not striving for a dull life or a mediocre life. We should all strive for a fabulous life.

It is a fact that you can have a group of people watch a movie, and at the end of the movie, you ask some simple questions wherein each person will have a different answer. When I was younger, I used to wonder how could that be. But as I got older, I quickly realized that each of us thinks individually, and it is our past experiences and opinions that cause us to view the world differently. It will likely prejudice the people we trust. The same picture means different things to different people because of life's experiences. What an astronaut thinks when he sees a picture of the planet from outer space is totally different from what the plumber thinks when he sees the same picture. This is also true about a day's events. There are those who get terribly upset when they find the plane flight is departing late, whereas others on that same flight take time to play games in the airport terminal or meet others. A great outcome about the critical elements is that you're going to gain confidence as you better understand and practice the critical elements. Part of the critical elements is being a decision-maker. But you're going to learn to make decisions logically and objectively versus emotionally. That type of decision-making will give you confidence and thus make you happier. You should understand that you carry with you past experiences that will also affect your viewpoint. Do not worry if your viewpoint differs from someone else's with a caveat or two. You must objectively consider the viewpoints of those that are in your core of support, and you must adhere to your own core principles. A person with an understanding of the critical elements is not going to make a purchase based on advertising. That person will establish an objective criteria before each purchase, and it will become very natural. Perhaps the objective criteria for a purchase will be exclusively on need. Perhaps it will be on emotion, and the person with an understanding of the critical elements will recognize the instant purchase is emotional but say to herself that it is what she works for. And that is a good thing. It's like purchasing a car. As I said, the person with a strong understanding of the elements is an independent thinker. Let's say that the person needs to get from point A (home) to point B (work) on a consistent basis. The independent thinker is first and foremost not worried about what others think. Stop trying to impress others.

Don't waste your time—not a moment of it—worrying about what the naysayers are thinking. Focus on those who love you. What would they support you doing? A part of understanding the critical elements is to learn to live your life for you. Now, when I make that statement, it is not absolute. It is absolutely true until you choose to have children. And when you find that lifelong partner, the meaning of *you* is actually the two of you. If you choose to have children, until they are adults, you have the responsibility of living life for them and you. That said, no one else is going to make your car payment or your mortgage payment. This is your life to live. I have never had someone ring my doorbell and give me money. I have never had my phone ring with a job offer I never applied for. Think of life objectively. If this person isn't paying for the car, then why would they have any say regarding my car? No one else is paying the mortgage, so put in the landscaping you want.

Let's assume a person with an understanding of the critical elements needs to purchase a car. You first think objectively for things like mileage, depreciation, and insurance costs. Is the car appropriate for where you live? If you live in a city with small parking spaces and parking garages, you don't want a large vehicle. If you live in an area subject to snow, you may need four wheel drive or front wheel drive. If you live in the country and haul things, you might want a pickup. But you also work hard for your earnings, and that certainly means a lot. You don't want to walk up to your car and not have it meet your needs. You're going to spend a lot of time with the car, so the emotional part needs to play a role, but it is limited compared to the objective measures like cost. Can you afford the nicer interior? Is it the color you want? The person with the critical elements can never be sold by a car salesman. The person with the critical elements realizes that the car salesman might be nice but is just doing a job. The benefit of a good salesperson is that she can answer all the technical and objective questions you have about the vehicle. But her job is to sell you a car. She is not your advocate or friend. That is not mean; it is just a fact. That doesn't mean a person who understands the critical elements can't buy the saleswoman a coffee at the coffee shop next door. It simply means the person with that knowledge is buying the coffee to make the saleswoman's day better, because the saleswoman can struggle just as anyone else, and kindness feels good.

We are bombarded with marketing techniques our entire lifetime. Some techniques are upfront and clear, like a commercial on TV. Others are not, like a sponsored article in a magazine about this great vacation, which is actually an advertisement. One of the things that is sold to us is this desire to retire. A person with the understanding of the critical elements to happiness never hears the word *work* as a bad word. In fact many people identify more with their work than with any other elements of their lives, meaning they feel value because their work proves they have value. When you meet someone for the first time, it is not uncommon for them to ask where you are from and what type of work you do. Let me say up front that I am not a retiring type of guy. I am not counting down the days to when I retire. And if I did retire from the position that earns me the most income now, I would likely change the work that I do. In fact, most folks who already understand the critical elements of happiness have more than one skill set. They can move into various positions with ease. Having more than one defined skill set is a great means of security.

I will likely die at my house when I'm installing a new front porch light or doing yet another home improvement project. And that is a good thing because it is something I find great joy in doing. I just hope it is not from electrical shock because I was not paying attention! These are projects I enjoy. I like having tasks so at the end of the day, I feel good about what I've accomplished. Sometimes I accomplish a goal using my hands. Sometimes it is with my mind, like learning a new language or looking at some financial documents. Sometimes it is with my heart, like making a call to a close friend who isn't feeling well, or volunteering to drive someone to an appointment. I am not the type of guy who can sit on sofa and watch TV all day and feel as though I had a good day. Quite the opposite. That is why a person with understanding also does not waste time on social media. A person with understanding also does not waste time taking hundreds of selfies. A computer display, no matter the size found on a smartphone or on a laptop, does not replace person-to-person interaction.

Let's assume you are with a group of five people at a park. Instead of playing volleyball, tossing a frisbee, or chatting about a travel destination they are all on their phones. What does that objectively say about what they think of you? You are here, right in front of them. Yet they choose to stay on that phone. Does that mean that you're not interesting? That you are not entertaining enough? It certainly says you are not important enough to them, such that they choose using an inanimate object instead of conversing with you. Are those the type of acquaintances you choose? I hope you would not consider them friends. And if you do that to someone else, what is the benefit? Look back at all your social media posts for the last year and objectively ask yourself if they have improved your life. Remember, that is just one side of the coin. Because the opposite side of the coin, which you also must consider, is the time spent on social media. That means it was time you did not spend doing something else. You chose not to learn the guitar, and thus you will never be in a band. You chose not to run, so your weight may be an issue. You chose not to call your grandfather, so you do not know what is going on in his life. You chose not to set a new goal. You chose not to study ahead in school to get better grades and greater knowledge. You chose not to gain further knowledge of any kind when knowledge is one of the key elements to a happy life. Instead, you pushed on a phone keypad all day instead of choosing all the other millions of choices in life. Was that a good decision? There is also an objective test to answer this question. Ask someone older than you. That will be your answer. There is a reason that you don't see old people in criminal gangs. You don't see them illegally racing cars in the streets. They are not in gangs or racing cars because it is a failed way of living. There is a reason you don't see older folks on their phones all day. That is because they understand the value of social interaction with others. They understand and actually feel the benefits of sharing a sandwich with someone versus eating alone and just using their phone. They know that phone use is not a critical element to happiness. Be an engineer and run a test. If you genuinely think a phone is a critical element to happiness, then try using your phone for an entire week without talking to anyone in person. See if you're happier at the end of the week. There is a huge difference between looking at pictures of a mountain and visiting that mountain. There is a huge difference between someone telling you what the beach is like and visiting the beach with someone. It is a rule in my family that phones are not allowed in sight during any meal. What is interesting is that when my incredible wife and I attend parties, we also never see phones. If someone must take a phone call for business, they apologize greatly and leave the room so as to not interfere in other's conversations. Think of that older person as a model for the proper use of a phone. Don't waste any more time trying to figure out what they know.

Be not only that good person but that great person. There is a creed that essentially reads, "There is a special breed of warrior ready to answer our nation's call. A common man with an uncommon desire to succeed. Forged by adversity, he stands alongside America's finest … I am that man." That is the creed of a US Navy SEAL. Be thankful first thing in the morning, the moment you wake up. You can't have an amazing week, an amazing year, or an amazing life without the proper attitude and the help of others—those who continue to watch out for your safety and your freedoms without asking you for anything in return. If you wake up some morning and don't feel motivated, perhaps you should change what you're doing and seek a position that serves others. There is a saying that the man who expects to be treated special will not appreciate as much as the humble man. When you are with others, don't just talk—converse. That means you need to listen. How will you impact someone in a positive way today? Is it to make someone laugh, or perhaps is this a day where you are a shoulder to cry on?

There is another wise saying: There is no mistake so great as thinking you will always be right. I have repeatedly stated that complete knowledge will always benefit you. It is an absolute statement. But limited knowledge can be harmful. As an example, if you are about to step off a curb and into a busy street, but you look in only one direction, you can easily be hit by something approaching from the opposite direction. But if you look both ways, you'll be aware of all pedestrians around you, bicyclists, people driving in the wrong direction, delivery vehicles, and those traveling in the proper direction. It is thus much safer to get a complete view of your surroundings before you step into the street. It is also true that knowledge is very much a part of happiness. For example, let's take the news. You must listen to news to help in your decision-making. But exactly what is news? The most accurate news is something that factually happened in the past. It is concise and clear reporting of a past event. It will not have an angle or slant or shade. I will repeat that: The most accurate news is something that factually happened in the past. Unless science or physics is involved, the news cannot predict the future. An example is financial news when a company reports its past quarterly earnings. The quarterly earnings are a fact, as is the current stock price. It is a fact who is the chief operating officer of the company. It is not news what the stock price will be next quarter, next month, or even the next hour. Anything reported regarding the future is just opinion. Exceptions to this are science based. I think the weather can be considered news because it is scientifically based and thus can give near-future results. This can also be true of earthquakes and volcanoes, but only in the near term.

Here is another example of what is and what is not news. As an engineer I can tell you that if in the past, you removed a critical structural element in a building, then it will, as a question of fact, fail. I could report it as news in a local paper if the public had an interest in that building. That is because of the sciences, such as material science and physics. Depending on what type of critical structural element you removed, the building may fail immediately, or it may fail when some stress or strain such as wind or rain is applied. In this limited sense, one could report as news that the building is going to fail, but one cannot report as news when it will fail. I listen to financial news to know exactly what happened with my investments today. But if you watch what is called the financial news, there is a ridiculous amount of opinion on the show. This is not news. It is labeled or packaged as news, but it is in fact just opinion. The same is true for political news. Political news is factually what happened in the past. But there is a tremendous amount of media personalities, who even label themselves as news experts, who render their opinion to a vast audience. I hope none of that vast audience is someone who has read this book, and I will objectively tell you why. Most everything that regards the future is not news. It is opinion. It is unlikely that opinion is going to make your day happier. To have a happier life, I submit you should turn off the opinion shows. Absolutely listen to the news of past events so that you can render an opinion for yourself. But the moment you hear something stated that is not from the past, you must immediately understand that it is just opinion. Also understand that quite often those folks on political news programs have only a limited knowledge on any one subject at most. They are not qualified to tell you what is going to happen in the future. And most certainly there is a slant or angle to a political news program. There is a famous song by John Mayer with the lyrics "And when you trust your television what you get is what you got, 'cause when they own the information, oh they can bend it all they want." If you watch only one program or one network, you are getting only the information they want to provide. Do you objectively believe that listening to someone else's opinion day after day makes you happiest? I submit it does not, given only so much time in a day.

Understand that your time is valuable. Is your time better spent listening to someone else's opinion on politics, or is it better spent trying to learn a new language, chatting with a neighbor, walking your dog in a park, playing a round of golf, or learning a new magic trick? If you want to relax in front of a television, try to find a program of value or particular interest to you. The best type of show would be one that reveals kindness. Hopefully, it is a show about true stories of kindness. My strong advice is to limit the amount of news you hear. Do you really need to watch the news every day? Is there perhaps a weekend summary show that can give you the general information needed? News is most often negative and opinionated. Because news is clearly biased, you should listen to various programs if you care to receive a balanced opinion. In general, because news is mostly negative, it does not make your life happier to view it often. In fact, I believe opinionated political news does not make one happier—it actually harms. Is your valuable time better spent reading social media or the Internet instead of calling your parents, advancing your career with some additional studies, spending time reading a book to your child, or perhaps building a tent with a child? Here is a simple, objective question. Look back on your life for exactly one year. In the past year, are you objectively happier for all the time you spend on social media? Are you objectively happier from watching politics on the television? And if so, you should be able to write down those positive experiences and memories. Is that total time better spent surprising your friend in your pajamas and going to a diner to eat pancakes just because you can? As a reminder, the more you think or act in a youthful manner, the more happiness you'll discover.

Let's take another form of knowledge: discussions with someone you trust. Let me give you an example of a discussion that I had with a young man before he went to college. I told him that if he ever goes to a large event, such as a college party or small music venue that gets overcrowded, he should be aware of his options and surroundings. He should always consider an emergency situation in that overcrowded venue. I told him about establishing a system to be repeated for his safety. When he first goes into the venue, he should look for exits. I told him panic was a bad thing, and panic happens if you don't have knowledge or experience with something. If he forgets to look for exits, but an emergency occurs, he should not act on impulse but should stop and think. I told him that in an emergency such as a fire, someone with a gun, or structural collapse, most everyone will run for the entrance. Why do they run for the entrance? Because that entrance is what they are most familiar with; that is what they have knowledge of. They have limited knowledge of where the front door is. They don't have that complete knowledge of the building. That limited knowledge is a weakness. How is this related to happiness? Knowledge isn't always about making you happier as it sometimes is about avoiding things that can make you or someone you love very unhappy. I told him that in most buildings, there is something like a table or a chair that can be used to not only break a window but to literally break through a wall. There are tools such as wiring or curtains that can be put together to form a rope or tether if you are on a higher floor. We had him write this discussion down on a piece of paper, in his own words, so he would remember it. When you have life-lesson discussions such as these, it should be written down at least once to better commit to memory. Another way to increase memory of such discussions is to have the discussion after you have a viewed an impactful program or movie regarding the same topic. As an example, if I had this discussion with this young man after reading a factual account involving loss of life at a nightclub, where patrons of a club lost their life because most ran for the entrance, it would be more committed to memory.

Life isn't about waiting for the waves to settle. It's about learning how to surf.

Chapter Eight

Educating Our Children: Possibly the Most Important Book *They* Will Ever Write

THIS CHAPTER IS ABOUT ESTABLISHING a system of trust so a parent can guide a child through their entire life. It was difficult to determine where to put this chapter in the book. Chronologically, it should be at the beginning because it involves children. In addition, this chapter is a critical chapter in possibly changing society by introducing a system that is not practiced to my knowledge. This is a chapter about establishing trust, and the term *establishing* requires a beginning. I am proposing a model of exactly where to begin and how. There is a possibility that a great number of people who read this book for the first time are younger adults without children. This chapter addresses establishing trust between a child and a parent and the monumental benefits it creates. As an adult, imagine all the benefits you could recognize if your child had absolute trust in every lesson you taught them. Communication is not just about a parent, for example, preparing a child for peer pressure in school. It also means a child can come home and tell a parent about the things that are worrying them in school. It also means a parent has to be a good listener and provide guidance to help their child to find their life passion(s). This system could be a critical element to prevent drug use, teen pregnancy, and even teen suicides, as well as misguided relationships and other poor choices. It's a system that includes teaching your child a system to overcome anger or frustration by using methods in this book. Teaching them that anger and frustration is wasted energy that never leads to happiness. That it feels terrible to be overly upset. That being upset solves nothing and can harm relationships as well as yourself.

One of the many great things when children are young is that they love to listen to and interact with their parents. Most children want to please their parents. A child is not only hearing what you say but also watching how you act. You are forming their understanding of what is right and wrong, what is acceptable and what is not. They are like a sponge ready to absorb everything they see and hear. Late adolescence, but prior to them becoming a teenager, is a perfect time to get a journal for them to write in. This is the perfect time to put in place a lifelong teaching tool.

A premise of this book is the acknowledgment that we want our children to be happier than us. When they are happy and healthy, we also benefit. We also factually know that a strong education leads to a higher likelihood of happiness. That education takes the form of both academics as well as foreknowledge of expected or possible life experiences. That education also takes the form of teaching your child about all the amazing opportunities in the world for them to do. Your child may never realize that they love downhill skiing or travelling to other countries if they have never been introduced to it. Perhaps they love music, animals, sewing, cooking, residential construction, roller coasters, designing clothes, parachuting or flying a plane. Perhaps they love interviewing others, acting, singing or painting. The earlier you can help them find their passion(s) the happier their life will be. So why don't most families have a system in place to ensure their children are educated regarding those life experiences? My parents did not have any system, but this book is a first step of hopefully making a change. When do parents have the greatest impact on teaching their children? When are the children most likely to follow a parent's guidance almost without questioning it? When they are younger and prior the teenage years. So why don't most families have a system in place to teach their children the value of hard work and kindness, to teach about peer pressure and the danger of drugs as well as the importance of academics? Why doesn't a parent talk precisely about what a true friend is and what a true friend is not? Why doesn't a parent talk almost endlessly about all the different opportunities that are available to their child to help that child find a true passion? How could a child or teenager have any idea of all the opportunities that are out there without guidance? In addition, does anyone believe that children are happier or better educated when they are given everything they think they want from their family? Did you notice that I stated what they think they *want*? Most children don't have the knowledge to know what they truly need. Everything more than what they need is just what they want. I fully agree that a parent is responsible for providing a child with everything they need. I do not agree that giving every child everything they want is a good thing. In fact, it can be very harmful.

Let me first address a system to ensure a child is educated regarding life experiences. Just as we want to add more happiness to our children's lives, we also want to reduce the negative factors. Why is that important? Having knowledge about a future event or experience will reduce the negative impacts of that future event or experience. I gave earlier examples such as a firefighter getting training by going into a staged fire before going into an actual fire. Essentially, every parent knows that a first or immature relationship is going to happen at a young age. Just like every parent knows that there is a high likelihood that their child may listen to a friend's guidance from high school before they listen to the parent. It is not uncommon for a parent to realize that their child's "friend" in high school may encourage their child to try drugs or sneak out of the house. Is this person a true friend? Absolutely not. But their child thinks that person is. A child without education does not know how to determine who is a true friend.

What does a parent do to change this well-known fact? Most do nothing until it's too late, or they hope it doesn't happen at all. Can this be changed? Absolutely. Then why does this continue to happen? I believe one answer is clear. The child does not know what they do not know but thinks they know everything. Any parent should know that this is highly likely to happen. Why? Because the parent had the exact same experience when they were in high school. It is not uncommon for a high schooler to believe that their high school "friend" cares more about them then their parent does. Why? Because parents fail every day to have the discussion about critical elements. That happens because parents don't know all the critical elements just as my parents did not. And of course, one of the critical elements is to have these types of discussions with your children as soon as possible. The time is right to begin private discussions with your children when you feel they are old enough to understand but prior the experience happening. When the parent begins with the first discussion (of many), it is critical that the parent have the child write this down in a journal. This sounds simple, but it is critical, so I will repeat it: When the parent begins to have these discussions with their child, they need to have the child, in their own handwriting, record the discussion in a journal.

It is important for the child to do the actual writing because the written word reinforces what your child hears. There can be a huge disconnect between what you tell someone versus what they hear or comprehend. By having your child write down the guidance, you can review every word and enhance the lesson and discussion. This is a very important journal for a child and may also remain important through adulthood. It is a journal that I suggest you title "Guidance from Those Who Love Me Most." Of course you can choose other titles, such as "Lessons for Life." Once you have chosen a title (perhaps your first discussion will be about the actual title), have your child write that down on the first page of the journal, if not the cover. You will have your child pull out this journal at certain time periods in the future, and the child should reread what they wrote with you. This will be very important *when* what they wrote matches with the actual experience. When this reread happens at a later date, it will open up a whole new discussion. And when the child recognizes the written things consistently come true, a greater trust will ensue. This trust system sounds simple, but it is critical. It must be in writing, and it must be repeated at different life stages and as issues arise. This system itself is a critical element. The system will clearly begin prior high school.

Imagine if your grandfather had established this system, and you had his guidance manual. You could also show your child your guidance manual and tell them how important it was for you. You would see how history will repeat itself regarding relationships but how it also changes regarding innovation. Your grandfather's journal might have lessons about the value of telling the truth, how to handle disappointment, working hard, and other valuable topics that can be passed down. Others' lessons might be era specific, such as how to be financially responsible by saving a penny in a glass jar and hiding it. Talk to your children about character. Teach them how to determine who is a true friend. Teach them the specific traits and signs that they have to possess to be a true friend. For example, if someone is telling your child to do something that you taught them is wrong then that person is objectively not a friend. Tell your child that they need only one friend, and it may be a brother or a sister. Tell your child never to settle for just anyone. And when your child understands these discussions your child should be writing these lessons down in their own handwriting.

Talk to them about their own character and about understanding the character of others. Tell them what you want their character to be like. Do you want them to be confident and hardworking yet humble? Give examples such as competing in sports in front of their school. What if your child is competing in a tennis tournament and loses in front of their entire class? Is that failing? No. Not if they did their best. That is character building. Experience is what you get when you don't get what you wanted. Have them understand that anyone who says anything negative to them about the loss is not a friend. You should make it clear that trying your best but losing is not failing; it is strengthening character. The loss of a single sporting event is minor to other experiences in life. When people show you their true colors by being derogatory or nasty, that is not a bad thing. It simply means you know the true character of that person. That person is not a true friend. Knowing good people from bad people is important in life. Don't let anyone tell you differently.

If you have a child who is a girl, there will quite likely be another girl in school who will tell her that she is ugly or fat, she talks funny, or some other mean statement. Teach her not to be hurt by that statement. She can actually understand it to be a positive event. When someone says something like that, she can objectively realize that the person cannot be trusted. That person cannot become a friend. She should simply smile, say *thanks*, and walk away. Nothing bothers a mean person more than someone who can simply ignore the negative statements. And nothing bothers a mean person more than someone who actually says, "thank you" and walks away. Remember, part of your lesson will be to tell your child how to react when that future event happens. You can actually act-out the event by pretending to be the "mean girl" in a pretend scenario. Change the lesson in any manner you need to help your child better understand the scenarios. You have to teach your children how to respond to mean children. Your child can be confident because you taught them to be prepared for these mean children. Similar things will happen as an adult. There will be individuals who try to attack your character, your work ethic, or your knowledge. Merely smile and walk away. Again, there is absolutely no benefit to having a conversation with someone who is that negative.

This book can act as a roadmap for discussions with your children, but it is certainly not limiting. Talk to your child about the critical elements of finding a lifelong partner. Talk to your child about friendships. Talk to your child about helping others and the reward that it brings. Teach your child what to expect in high school, in vocation school, on the school bus, on the playground, and in graduate school. Try to prepare your child for as many life experiences as you can, because knowledge is instrumental to better outcomes. Talk to your child about your own job and whether it is rewarding to you and why. Help your child discover things that may become a passion for both her work and her free time. Talk to your children about failure, anger, envy, jealousy, worry, and anxiety. Talk to your child about depression and say that it is nothing to be ashamed about or to hide. Talk to your child about forgiveness, kindness, politeness, being humble, and being helpful. If your child is going to attend college, then talk to your child about the college experiences ahead of them attending college. And when you talk to your child about school be specific. Do not just ask "how was school today". Ask who they played with. Ask who they sat with at lunch. Ask about each class and if anyone is disruptive in class. Ask who is their best friend and be certain to ask why. Ask what was their favorite class and why. Ask what was their favorite moment of the day and why. Find out who is their favorite teacher and make it a point to meet all of their teachers and ask prepared specific questions.

Before we get into the specific life lessons that you need to discuss with your children, let me give you some examples. Imagine being a brand-new paramedic and being told to do your best to try to save lives without any training. Would you ever send someone into an emergency situation without any training? What would that first experience be like? Would you ever think to throw your child into a pool without a swimming lesson? Of course not! Would you ever think to put your child on a two-wheeled bike without any experience of training wheels? Then why would you think it was okay to send your child to high school without first discussing some of the many possible things he may experience and witness? Why wouldn't you first have a discussion about choosing the right friends? After all, you know many of these life lessons because you have already experienced many of these situations. Knowledge or preparation is a tremendous benefit to both children and adults. It's almost never too early to start learning. And when it's time to begin some of these discussions, your child should have that journal to write down what you've talked about. When you have a serious topic to discuss with your child, it may be best to start with a movie or production similar to the topic that will set the mood for the discussion. As an example, if you're about to talk to your child about not wanting to grow up too fast, you might consider watching the movie *Big*. If you're about to talk to your teenager about using their phone while driving, I suggest you research a production, and prescreen it before you watch it together, that involves a teenager on a cell phone. Having that production will help establish the seriousness of the discussion instead of bringing it up out of the clear blue. Another option, when you want to have a serious conversation with your child, is to do so during quiet time together, such as during a bike ride, fishing, or camping. Talk about driving with other teens, driving at night, and not wearing a seat belt. Talk about the dangers of speeding, distracted driving, drowsy driving, and impaired driving. All these lessons should be written down. As a parent, you also need to prepare your child for fundamental tasks in life. How to apply for credit. How to mow a lawn. How to make a bed. How to replace an electrical fixture. How to balance a checking account. How to negotiate. How to do the laundry. How to clean the bathroom. How to cook. How to organize. How to negotiate. How to survive if you get lost. If items such as these are written down in their trust journal will this help to create a greater bond of trust? The clear answer is *yes*. This also means your young child, and even an adult child, will also be able to come to you with things that hurt or bother them because of that trust.

When do you start with a life experiences journal? The time is right when your child is about to have an experience and you are aware of possible bad outcomes. Other elements of this book, such as finding a passion, can start at the earliest age. Expose your child to as many activities and interests as you can think of. What if you find your child, at the age of three, is amazing on a piano? What if she is amazing in chess? What if she has a great interest in painting? What if she is amazing at photography? Will your child be a geologist, veterinarian, astronomer, astronaut, painter, puzzle designer, clothes designer, engine technician, photographer, appliance technician, kitchen designer, singer, hair stylist, makeup artist, or entrepreneur? Bring your child to the zoo and see whether they have an interest in birds, elephants, or the ecosystem of otters. Have your child help you in the garden to see if they have an interest in horticulture or cooking with fresh vegetables. These examples are literally endless. Your child's dreams can be as large as this planet, but only if you help them dream. A child has no idea what is out there. They think only in terms of your yard, your street, and their school. Show them video of astronauts in space and documentaries on how satellites work. My parents never told me all the opportunities that were available to me; I had to learn on my own. Your child is thirsting for direction, but they don't know it. You should be providing that direction. You can have a discussion about how friendships in middle school will end when your child moves on to a different high school. You should have the discussion about hormones for both a girl and a boy and what changes to their bodies they are going to experience. You should definitely have a discussion about having a first love and how they are going to feel. The discussion will include the expectation that it will likely end. Therefore the discussion will include what that ending will feel like. When it comes to relationships, you should establish your core principles with your children to make their decision-making easier. Remember, this is all being written down by your child. The more you are correct about things that they read in their journal, the more trust you're going to establish. Although I can throw many other lessons out there, it is hard for me to create a complete list because every child is different. If a child is competing in a sport or trying out for a team, you must talk about it first. The team is going to experience a loss. They may not make the team. But every parent should have a list, and every child should be writing in a journal about the guidance the parent is providing.

Equally important to writing down guidance regarding expected life experiences is instilling in your child the importance of academics. Encourage your child's curiosity. It is a shame that many of us, as we get older, stop questioning. Curiosity is a great thing to cultivate. Never stop asking questions. By academics, I do not mean that every child must go to college. The happiest life is one in which you have loved the most. A great portion of your life is your work. It would be fabulous to earn a living from something that you love to do. A parent can help to guide a child to do something they love. If a child loves working with their hands, perhaps you can help them learn about the air-conditioning trade. Perhaps they have an interest in business and thus classes in business is best for them. Perhaps they have an interest in cooking, and they can be guided to being a chef with classes in the culinary arts. Maybe they love sports, so they want to get a degree in sports management, physical therapy, or personal training. The opportunities are almost endless in every field. Do your children have an interest in the weather? Perhaps meteorology is exciting. Do they have an interest in talking to others and are excited about mystery games? Perhaps some classes in journalism or criminal justice are a good place to start. Do they have an interest in travel? Perhaps hotel management would pique their interest; they could work with an international hotel chain and travel the world with their job. Your parents likely never told you about all the opportunities that were out there. Mine certainly did not. But that doesn't mean you can't bring that excitement to your child's dreams.

The earlier you can find a passion in your child, the easier it is for you to guide them in the direction to help them the most. That said, every parent must instill the importance of a child excelling in academics all through at least high school. Of all the guidance and understanding you can provide for a child, this is by far the most critical. It is unquestionable fact that academic knowledge is a critical element to happiness. You must instill in your child that knowledge plus action overcomes every hurdle put before them. You could be brilliant, but if you don't apply yourself, if you have no motivation, then you will not succeed. Someone who is motivated and has knowledge transcends all roadblocks in life. I will scream from the rooftops to any younger person out there that you can accomplish literally anything if you focus on education. Aristotle said, "The roots of education are bitter, but the fruit is sweet." Nelson Mandela said, "Education is the most powerful weapon which you can use to change the world." The only absolute way to overcome every obstacle placed in your way is to seek the best education you can find. Don't stop that education until you have achieved at least an associate degree or the highest level of education you can achieve in a field you are passionate about.

All of us have heard someone blaming others for their position in life. It's been said that the only true disability in life is a negative attitude. Blaming others, whether true or not, will get you nowhere. Be assertive for yourself. Fight for that education. And the higher the education, the better. Also, a diverse education is highly advised. If you could be an expert in plumbing and electricity and heating and air-conditioning, you will never need to worry about earning a good living. And if you enjoy the trades, you'll never feel like it is work. I can repeat examples all day. Education is the answer for earning a good living with a focus on learning about something you are passionate about. Academic knowledge transcends where you live, how you were raised, your economic situation, your nationality, the color or your skin, and whether you are tall or short, slender or heavy, fast or slow. Where you come from does not determine where you can go and what you can achieve. Tell your child to never discount themselves. Teach your children to ignore or get rid of any victim mentality. Do not accept it; it is like giving up on life. It is poisonous. What you were born with, where you were born, or whom you were born to does not matter. Teach them that their starting line is just different. But tell them you know that their finish line is going to be fabulous.

Try to give your child a thirst for knowledge, both academic knowledge and knowledge of their passion. But above all, encourage them to seek academic knowledge. A child who excels in the sciences will have the world at their feet. You should research what career paths offer the greatest opportunities for your child consistent with their interests. Perhaps a career in a computer field or medical field. As you know, my degrees are in Engineering. According to numerous analyses, engineering is the most common undergraduate degree for Fortune 500 CEOs. Engineering teaches a systematic way to approach problems, as

I do with this book. With an understanding of the math and sciences, you can choose whatever path you want in life. You can become a professional surfer and be great in understanding business or finances (math). You can be a marathon runner and create methods to cool your body or create a clothing that wicks moisture faster than any other material. Perhaps you'll think of a better way to deliver nutrition to runners during the actual event. Perhaps you'll develop a better shoe. The academic training of an engineer has your child thinking of ways to not only solve problems but also understand that a problem even exists. If you owned a company and are looking to hire, would you consider an engineer who was on the dean's list? If you were a computer company, would you consider a student who graduated with honors in computer science? If you were a hospital, would you want to have in your program a medical student who is at the top of her class? If you were a college, would you want a student who is a member of the national honor society applying to your university? Every parent should instill in their child a simple phrase to remember: Knowledge is power. Knowledge gives you freedom to choose a path in life that is most exciting to you because you have skills others need.

A child who barely makes it through high school is faced with a lifelong disadvantage compared with a child who academically excelled through high school. This needs to be critically understood by your child before they ever start high school. Instill in your child the need to excel and do their best in school. Did your parents give you any learning tools regarding school? It is important that you teach your children how to learn, meaning how to be the best student and how to learn the most in a given period. A person who knows the critical elements realizes that if you don't know the right question to ask, you'll never get the right answer. What this means is that your child should be prepared. Did you tell your child that to excel in school, they should always read ahead of the lesson? If your child is sitting in class and hearing about algebra for the very first time, it may be intimidating. But if your child reads ahead and perhaps asks for your help in algebra, then when they hear that lesson in school, they will be less intimidated. They will be better prepared. That allows for better listening and comprehension. It allows your child to ask more intelligent questions because they are now prepared. This is a simple yet incredibly helpful learning method. This is the exact same analogy of the paramedic being prepared for his first emergency situation. If you are not prepared, you don't even know what to ask. By reading the material ahead of time, a student can be a better listener and take better notes on the finer points they didn't understand when reading the subject matter on their own. Even this fundamental and repeatable system gives your child a leg up with respect to students who aren't prepared. It reduces stress and makes learning more enjoyable. Have your child get the reading material before class begins, and read ahead of each lesson. Make it a rule, presented in a very positive way, that they should not be learning about material for the first time only when a teacher is presenting it.

Also make it clear to your child to share any concern they have at school because even the smallest concern can harm the learning process. And do not leave it up to your child to raise the concern even though you have asked them to do so. You need to ask questions on a consistent basis and ask the questions in different ways to make sure you are getting honest answers. One day you may ask broadly, "How was school today?" Follow it with more specific questions such as, "What did you learn in math class?" Then get even more specific with questions such as, "Is the sun hitting your desktop, making it too bright?" Another more specific question may be, "Did your friend John, who is good in math, ask the teacher any questions?" That is a way to see whether your child is also paying attention. You need to ensure your child is given the best opportunity to learn. If your child has difficulty in seeing the blackboard, it will harm learning significantly because their brain is working to focus on what is written on the blackboard while the teacher is presenting, and thus they are missing parts of the lesson. If a child does not have the correct materials to record a lesson, it will harm the learning process. If your child is hungry during class, such that they begin to drift off and think about lunch, it will harm the learning process. If your child has difficulty in hearing, it will harm the learning process because the brain is once again trying to catch up to what is being said. If your child is worried about their safety or their relationship with others at the school, it will harm the learning process. Imagine there is a mean student who sits behind you child and pokes your child on the back of the neck, shoulder, or arm. That will dramatically adversely affect their ability to learn. In the same regard, if there is a friend who sits behind or next to your child and wants to be silly, they will distract your child from learning. Thus I suggest that your child not sit directly next to their friends. I also suggest that you tell your child that given a choice they should always sit at the front of the class. As a parent, you should visit your child's school at least once to directly observe, at a distance, your child in each classroom. Any measure of stress harms the learning process. The happier a child is, the more confident a child is about a subject, and the easier it is for them to learn. These are fundamental facts, and these are critical elements for you as a parent to practice to give your child the happiest experience during schooltime when they are away from you. Your children may have amazing teachers, but even amazing teachers don't know your child like you do.

Let me give you another system to reinforce values and the importance of knowledge with children and young adults. This system should be practiced at dinnertime in every household. For ease of understanding, I will call it the mealtime system. One of the strongest ways to maintain the family bonds is to practice eating dinner together. Family bonds are very important to children because they impart security, and a child needs to feel secure. Eating meals together as a family should be a priority, just as it should be for married couples. If this mealtime system can't be practiced at dinner, then make it brunch or some other meal. First of all, there are rules for the system. The first rule is that no phones are allowed at the dinner table. Dinner is all about recognizing the importance of everyone at the table. That means part of the system is to have everyone at the table speak and everyone at the table listen to what is being said. You cannot be listening or speaking if your attention is somewhere else, such as looking at a phone. The only exception to the no-phone rule is if one of the family members cannot attend the meal and is joining the meal via the phone. Another rule is that you are allowed to invite guests. If there are guests, you want them to also participate in the tradition. The hope is that your mealtime tradition will then be shared with other families via your guests, and the guest will also understand the importance of sharing each of our individual gifts. The next rule is to select a day when academics are a priority. It may be once a week, perhaps every Sunday evening. On that academic's night, everyone at the table has to speak for a set period of time, without interruption, about an academic topic that is new to everyone else at the table. You may set a minimum period of time or a maximum period of time; as an example, it may be a targeted amount of two minutes. The speaker is going to teach something to everyone else at the table. This reinforces the value of education and it reinforces the value of each individual at the table. Then questions can follow before it proceeds to the next person. A further benefit of this system is that your children are going to learn to be a good speaker. This is a very valuable skill set. You hope it will also teach confidence in place of any shyness. Another benefit is that your children will learn to become good listeners. You should encourage them to ask questions after each presentation. Your children will also learn to be prepared by likely doing research on the topic they are about to discuss. Are they going to talk about the phases of the moon? Perhaps the relationship between voltage and amperage and resistance? Are they going to illustrate how to wire a three-way switch? Are they going to teach everyone about centrifugal force on a merry-go-round? Perhaps they will talk about how an airplane wing causes lift. Perhaps everyone will learn about the highest mountains in each country, or the world record for diving the deepest and how it was done. There are endless topics.

The value in the tradition, in the system, is to reinforce as a family the importance of knowledge and education. What you may not yet realize is that this simple system will have many more positive benefits for everyone at the table beyond the few I already mentioned. I also suggest that you add other mealtime traditions, like perhaps having an evening of strictly current events. Better yet, you can have a meal where everyone must talk about a company to invest in. That way, each family member will learn how to evaluate a company. How many shares were traded last week? Did a board member sell any shares? What is the revenue and earnings before interest, taxes, depreciation, and amortization? You can talk about creating a system that you think best establishes whether you should invest. If your family is highly interested in sports, perhaps you could add a sports night once a month, or even an "open topic" meal or "best joke" night.

I also suggest creating a family tradition of spending at least one holiday together for at least one meal, no matter the age of your children. That holiday meal should include traditions that keep the family bond together. Perhaps that holiday could be your dad's birthday or Valentine's Day, or perhaps it is June 20, one of the longest days of the year in the northern hemisphere for maximum daylight. You can create your own traditions to focus on your family priorities. These priorities can vary with endless possibilities year over year, or they can remain the same. Perhaps one year you will plant a tree in memory of someone. Perhaps each year you will have a surfing contest or 3K run. Perhaps you'll have a scavenger hunt. Whatever the tradition, you should try to incorporate activities that focus on each of the family members in an equal manner.

In addition to the guidance journal, you should also memorialize, by reducing the discussion to a written document, when you have discussions with your *teenage* children or when they are young adults. I call these household agreements and recommend titling the document as such. This written agreement helps avoid any arguments. Both parties are clear upon what is agreed upon. You can point to the written document, or household agreement, with both your signatures. A perfect example is having the car home by 11:00 p.m. Of course, the document has to have penalties included if the agreement is not met, so if the car is not home by eleven, there are consequences. Again, this is a very valuable learning tool. In the real world, everyone enters into written contracts. It might be a rental contract, a mortgage, a bank note, a loan document, or a waiver to ride a zip line. The consequences may range in penalties. If you do not have the car home by 11:00 p.m., you will be restricted from driving the car for a full month. If you do not maintain a B average in every class, you will be required to take summer school. On the positive side for each A in school you earn, we will put $250 toward your college fund. A child should understand that college is about competing for the best grades and being on the dean's list. It is not about fun and entertainment. Of course, this should also have been understood during their high school years. A college student should be trying to learn as much as they can academically while they are there. Learning is the priority. Only if they manage their time well can they go to the football game or wresting match. The reality is that each student is competing with other students to get the best job and learn the most. Again, put important things in writing. You may have a household agreement that states if they are arrested on campus, that you will no longer pay a share of their college. As a side note, notice that I stated "a share of" their college. I think every child should be responsible for a share of their college expenses to understand the value of the education. Perhaps if your child is caught speeding a second time or running a red light, they will not be allowed to drive the car for a month, and they will now need to pay their own insurance. By having these understandings in writing, it reinforces the importance of these issues. More importantly it establishes an agreement and avoids arguments. Your child can see in black and white the result of any action.

Changing the topic slightly, just because someone is paranoid and thinks that there is a person out to get them, that doesn't mean they're wrong. Your child should understand that a sense something is wrong is almost always right. According to research, most people make up their minds about others within two minutes, and these snap judgments are surprisingly accurate. People still need to trust their gut and rely on instinct when a snap decision is needed or they feel uneasy about their circumstances. Make sure your child trusts their instincts during high school and college, or anytime they are away from you. Tell them that you will pick them up any time if they feel it is not safe to get into a friend's car. Tell them that you trust them to make the right decision and that you support that decision. You can also now see the benefit of starting early with the guidance journal and the trust it brings between you and your children.

I will tell you a true story from when I was a young adult to reinforce the importance of this trust. There was a father who was very strict with his son. He made statements such as, "You had better not even come home if you damage my car." He was also stern regarding the time his son had to be home. He said things such as, "You had better be home by 11:00 p.m., or don't ever think of using my car again." It so happens that this family lived in a neighborhood wherein the entrance of their neighborhood was off a single-lane state road. It had a northbound side and a southbound side divided by a dashed white line to allow passing. The state road did not have a shoulder along this portion and was elevated with ditches on either side for water drainage. The state road was almost perfectly straight for many miles along this section, which allowed for the passing line down the center.

The son had borrowed his dad's car one night and left his friend's house at the last minute to make it home on time. As the son was heading north, a drunk driver, with his high beams on, was heading south on that same road. The son was within a mile of the entrance to the family's neighborhood. The son could see the drunk driver because the drunk driver was swerving dramatically from the southbound lane into the northbound lane and back again, and the road was very straight. We also know this because a police officer was behind the drunk driver with his lights on and could see the northbound car, driven by the son, trying to avoid a collision by moving his car opposite that of the drunk driver. But at the last moment, the drunk driver switched lanes and hit the northbound car, driven by the son, almost head-on. It killed the boy.

Why didn't the boy stop his car to reduce the impact? Was he worried about getting home on time and knew he was so close to the entrance to the neighborhood? Since there were no driveways along that stretch of road, why didn't he drive off the road to make sure he would avoid such an impact? Was he worried that his father would go ballistic if he damaged the car? Was he worried his father would not believe why he had driven off the road? The father could almost not bear the loss of his son, but now it was too late. Do not be one of those people who have to experience a tragedy before they look at life differently. Make sure your children know you cherish them and trust them. Make sure your child understands that the car is of little value. Perhaps sharing this exact story will help.

When it comes to being a parent or guardian, is it important that you are the best? No. It is important that you are there as much as possible, and when you are, you'll be the best quite naturally. This is where quantity is more important than quality. How many times have you lain next to your child and read them a bedtime story? The benefit of lying next to your child is that the sense of touch is very important and is valuable at relating trust. Imagine reading a bedtime story from a chair on the other side of the room. Compare it to your child leaning against you while you read. Which is more comforting? The other benefit of reading bedtime stories is that it encourages your children to read themselves. This will benefit them for the rest of their lives. They understand that stories can provide all sorts of emotions. Stories can provide comfort, mystery, tension, excitement, trust, and even scary moments. But remember to limit the scary moments when it comes to bedtime stories! Remember all of your senses, so you might want to add some sounds of the ocean if you're reading them a story about being at the beach, or sounds of rain if the story takes place in the rain. With today's computers, you can import almost any sound. Don't be a mediocre storyteller. Strive to be an amazing storyteller so the memory lasts for your children. You don't have to do this with every story, but it might be really cool when there is a sleepover! As a very important side note, although you might find it difficult at the end of a long day to read that bedtime story, you should realize what an amazing gift you are experiencing. Do not take any of these moments for granted. Remember this lesson in life: The more you take for granted, the less you'll appreciate. One day, you may wish to have back those bedtime reading moments. Take time yourself and think about how lucky you are to have this happy, healthy, and attentive child beside you. Spend time riding a bike with your kids, play tennis, play golf, and watch them do gymnastics. You will find that sharing time with your children, even without speaking, will form a greater bond between you. The more time you spend, the greater the bond. Time together will also further the feeling of trust.

What an amazing world this could be if we could all guide our children away from depression, anxiety, drugs, additive behavior, and early pregnancy by preparing them for all of life's experiences. At the same time, we can guide our children down an amazing path so they love what they do, find lifelong friends, and meet someone who loves them without limits. I also need to raise another important factor regarding children. Because you elected to have children, you took on a responsibility of raising your child to become a confident, happy, and trustworthy adult. First of all, as I have said earlier, never take anything for granted. Having a child should certainly not be taken for granted. Having a child is a gift. There are millions of woman who cannot have children. You may be able to have only one. This decision to have a child also means your priorities must change. Your child needs your protection. They need to feel safe and secure. This is a good time to bring up the fact that many of us feel comfort in what we are familiar with. Many don't consider that change could be exciting. For example, if you were born in a certain city you tend to stay in that area or return to it. If you are familiar with a certain store, credit card, app, car brand, or restaurant, you will tend to repeat their use. If people are familiar with a certain politician, a majority will tend to reelect that politician without giving a newcomer an opportunity. If you are familiar with a certain neighborhood, you will stay in that neighborhood. When you have a child, all of that changes. It does not matter what you are familiar with. Your priority is to provide your child with the best life. That means you should move to where the best schools are located. I noted earlier in this chapter that academic knowledge can overcome any and all roadblocks in life. You need to provide your child with the highest quality of academic education you can find. That means you are seeking a highly ranked school not only in your state but nationally. Therefore, as an adult it makes no difference that you love living in the city if the best schools are in a rural area or in another state. You must understand that there are millions of adults who have moved their families from another country to create a better life. It is selfish for adults to think they cannot move out of a neighborhood, much less a city, for the benefit of their children. You need to find a home where your child can go out and play with essentially no concern for their safety. I fully understand that this may require sacrifices. You might have to move into a smaller apartment. You might have to get a used car. You need to think in terms of introducing your child to as many experiences as possible to help them find a passion. Bring them fishing, to the zoo, to the park to fly a kite, to a museum to understand art, or to a building site to see structural steel. Enroll them in sports, go to free music concerts, and teach them what a dentist does (okay, hopefully you can delay that one). Be directly involved with their school to make sure your child has selected kind friends. And when you are sitting in the bleachers at graduation, you will realize that the changes that were required because of your child were fabulous for you as well. You will learn to welcome change. You will see that change can bring you greater happiness. In fact, the lack of change never brings happiness. As I mentioned in chapter 5, life is more exciting when you make an effort to try something new. You should embrace change instead of desiring mostly things that are familiar. I also mentioned in chapter 4 that one of the critical elements of happiness is the ability to give. What better person is there to give your guidance, your love, your help, your support, and your listening ear than your own child?

Chapter Nine
Health of Your Body

CAN ONE BAD DAY PULL you down longer than one amazing day can keep you content? If so, you need to change the way you think. You need to look at each day anew. You need to learn to forget about the past. It is rare that thinking about negative events can benefit you. The exceptions are those negative events that teach you a lesson going forward so they are not repeated. To keep the positive attitude, I cannot recommend enough the need to properly exercise. A critical factor to happiness is indeed health—physical health as well as mental health. There is definitely an interconnection between mental health and physical health. Keeping a healthy mind is just as important as a healthy body. Learning and discovery is what makes us happy at any age. Mental happiness is as critical to your well-being and quality of life as food and water is to your physical being.

Thus, you need to take time each day to focus on your physical and mental health. You need an objective plan to keep yourself fit both physically and mentally. On the mental side, you should take breaks in the day to enjoy that cup of coffee or at least those coffee breaks. Take your mind off of work and relax doing something different, or simply close your eyes and rest. By *something different* I mean catch up on sports, write a love letter, listen to music, meditate, do a crossword puzzle or anything else you enjoy. This is true whether you love your work or work to earn a living. Perhaps it's a phone call to a partner or friend. Perhaps its learning a new word. Perhaps it's taking your pet for a walk. If you ever feel depression or anxiety you need to establish an objective plan to stop those feelings. I made clear in this book that education and discovery is critical to happiness. I also made clear that exercise can make you feel both mentally stronger and physically stronger. So if you are feeling depressed try taking your mind off of those thoughts and focus on something that takes your full attention both physically and mentally. For example, it is highly unlikely that you could remain depressed when you are focused on learning a new country line dance. It is highly unlikely that you can remain depressed when you are exerting yourself in a physical manner for an extended period of time like a distance run or swim. It is highly unlikely that you could remain depressed when you are focused on trying to learn something that you find exciting like a new language or perhaps knitting or fly-fishing or couples tennis. In a similar manner, I have never met anyone that thinks I feel "happy, happy, happy" as they run for relatively long distances. When you speak to a distance runner they will tell you that it helps them to calm their mind. If you have a feeling of loneliness then confront it. How do you objectively overcome that feeling? There are lots of people who feel lonely. One way is to seek out and gain group experiences. Act in a community play. It takes lots of practice and thus lots of interactions with other folks. This is just one example. Don't just sit around and do nothing, but instead choose to act. I mean it literally. Maybe local community acting will become a passion. Older individual medical studies show that an individual will live longer with socialization versus those that are in isolation. These studies objectively prove that socialization, friendship, are critical elements to a happy life. There is not a single study that I am aware of that states that those with more material items lives longer. These studies can be expanded to make clear that happiness and one's positive mental health is gained more by acquiring more "relationships and experiences" versus acquiring more "things".

Another critical element to happiness is the need to feel strong health wise and have a great level of energy to be at your best. If you are not at your best physically, how can you participate in a passion that includes sports? If you are not at your best mentally, how can you perform at your best at work or at a passion that is mentally challenging? For me, my health routine includes three consistent elements: strength training, cardio training, and stretching. I do each of these elements every other day, and I ensure that I do the cardio portion for at least twenty minutes. I can tell you with certainty that this routine enhances my overall happiness. I notice a higher level of mental acuity when I exercise. I feel good about my body type. This routine allows me to maintain a high level of energy. I know I have a higher level of mental acuity because I can measure it objectively in some of the puzzle exercises I do. For example, I will notice a reduction in the speed of doing a puzzle if I am tired mentally. I see a similar result when I travel great distances. Flying tends to give me fatigue. If I pull out a puzzle during that long flight, I will notice a slower-than-usual ability to solve the puzzle. Think of it as an objective measure of my cognitive skills, like a drunk driver being tested objectively for their cognitive abilities. If I fail to work out for a week, I will objectively notice a change in my energy levels; they will be reduced. This may sound counterintuitive, but the more consistent I am at exercising, the more energy that I have. I am spending energy to gain more energy. I find it enjoyable to maintain a high level of activity even on vacation. I was once in the hospital and thus stuck in a bed for a week. I definitely noticed a reduction in ambition, drive, energy, and strength during that week. That is because I know my energy level from lifelong experience.

It is difficult to be happy on days you don't feel well. There is an adage that states, "Feed a cold, starve a fever." I do neither. I have what may be an unusual solution for when I start to get a headache, body ache, or head cold. I have found that if I run or work out hard for at least twenty full minutes, so my body is sweating and my heart is really pumping, my symptoms disappear. I am certainly not a doctor, and thus I do not know how it will work for everyone, but it certainly works for me. You have to be self-motivated to even consider going for a run when you have a headache, nausea, or cold symptoms. It's sometimes tough for me, but I do it every time because it consistently has proven to work for me. Those first few blocks are sometimes extra tough, but once my heart starts pumping and I start sweating, I can feel my energy coming back and my headache disappearing. I have to assume that what I am doing, in objective terms, is self-elevating my body temperature and thus killing whatever bug I have. Otherwise I am perhaps accelerating healing by increasing my blood circulation. It is kind of like hydrotherapy, where people increase their body temperature by taking a hot bath. I think I also get extra benefits by running or working out if I feel a cold coming on. I not only increase my body temperature by running but also increase my blood flow and air exchange in the fresh air. I objectively consider whether the results are partly caused by my strong belief in the outcome, and I am certainly fine with that. If I can mentally convince my body to heal itself so I continue to feel great, that is okay. A lot of folks want to take a headache pill and perhaps go to bed. I do not. My energy level is maintained, and my symptoms disappear with exercise. It makes logical sense because, conversely, if I sat around on a couch for a week, I would likely feel reduced energy due to lack of movement. If you are a person who is creative, are you more creative after sitting on a couch or after going on a brisk walk? I submit your body is telling you what is best for you both mentally and physically.

I suggest that if you are not proud of your body type, you should start doing something about it right away. As I mentioned earlier in the book, you will be a happier person by setting goals throughout your entire life. If you are not happy with your current living condition a goal is to change it. But you need to be specific as to what steps are needed to accomplish broad goals. One immediate goal may be to change your body type. Understand that the goal of changing your body type is far too broad a goal. I am a huge supporter of having huge goals. But you need to break down such large goals into more specific goals or milestones. As you reach those specific goals you may want to reward yourself. If you lose ten pounds, you'll reward yourself with a new bike, a new haircut, or a weekend getaway. Perhaps the loss of ten pounds will be reward enough to keep you motivated and on track for the next milestone. Set an overall goal, and as always, attach a timeline or date on your calendar to achieve each milestone step. Perhaps there will be multiple facets to each milestone. Like if the goal is to lose weight there may be an exercise component as well as a diet component. Be specific about each component to achieve the overall goal. I can assure you that as you improve your overall health, you will discover other benefits. Did you know that poor health even effects your ability to sleep, and to sleep more soundly? Again, it makes logical sense. Compare the sleep you would get if you have ever done a strenuous task, such as moving to a new house, versus one where you watched television. Moving all those boxes, furniture, and miscellaneous items may get you worn out, and you'll sleep soundly. Whereas after a day where you watched television, went through your mail, and chatted on the phone leaves your mind wandering with no physical exhaustion. Which process would you recommend if you were having problems sleeping? Would you recommend an exercise routine or binge-watching a television program? Sleep deprivation has been linked to a variety of health issues such as weight gain, high blood pressure, negative impacts on short- and long-term memory, mood changes, and poor balance, among other side effects. Thus, exercise is objectively great for you.

I stated that setting goals in your entire life will make you happier. This never changes, even with age. I also suggested an immediate goal may be changing your body type. But the types of goals are as endless as you desire. Realize that not all goals will be reached, but you'll feel better in trying to reach those goals. Perhaps a goal is straight A's in school, getting into veterinarian school, or not getting any cavities. Whatever the goal is, the only way to achieve that goal is to start. If you do not take a first step toward something, no matter how small that step, you will never begin the journey toward the goal. If the goal is large, then break it down into smaller achievable goals. If your goal is to lose thirty pounds by June 30 (goals should always be written down and have a specific timeline), then start with losing one pound this week, or lose five hundred calories a day. Then figure out how to lose those calories. Is it by more exercise or changing your diet? Just start. You have to start, or you can't accomplish your goals. It's just like chapter 1 of this book, where I gave the financial analogy of saving money. Start by investing that first dollar. If you don't start with the first dollar, you'll never save. And start tomorrow. If you don't do it tomorrow, then tomorrow will be just like yesterday, and the rest of your life will be filled with yesterdays and goals not reached. Learn to change the course of your life. Get that calendar, write down your goals, and start. Each one of these goals requires tasks to be performed to reach the goal, and that is what will keep you active. That is a great thing.

Let me give you an example. I read a news article about a famous country singer. He said he was in the best shape of his life and proud of it. The country star talked about his values and body transformation over the years. "My whole life, I've lived according to one key value. I guess I've done so from an early age, when I wanted so fiercely to get beyond my circumstances," he wrote. "That value is, Be ready. Be primed for opportunity when it shows up, because it will come once, it will move on quick, and if you're not ready to make the shot, your whole destiny can change in a heartbeat. Miss that moment, and you'll live the rest of your life wondering just how much of your potential never played out. Focusing on my physical health hasn't just made my body healthier, it's made me healthier at every level. Moving daily and exercising regularly was a pebble that set off a ripple effect, improving the way I eat, sleep, relate to others, and show up both personally and professionally. It made me a better person to be around." Does any of this sound familiar? I hope that objectively makes my point. I submit that to reach your full potential of happiness, there is a physical component that is critical. Your health routine will affect many facets of your life. If you have a special someone you should team up with that partner for motivational support. Get into a healthy routine.

Even if you are in a healthy routine, there are also environmental factors that can affect you, like the occupation that you work in, the food you eat, and even the area you live in and how the weather is in that area. For example, I find it difficult to live in a city with several days of rain in a row or lots of overcast days. I personally need the sun to feel energized. I also find it difficult to live in an area with minimal daylight in the winter. Again, this is very personal to me, and this does not mean that northernmost or southernmost locales are not fabulous places to live for others. I simply know my physiology. Perhaps it is because I was born in a warmer climate farther south. Whatever the reason, if you have the option to choose where you can live, I submit that you will likely be happier in a location where you can enjoy the outdoors the most. Happiness is not found sitting in one room or even a large house. Happiness is found being with others. If you are a person who loves to snow ski or a person who loves to surf, that passion should affect where you live for your overall happiness. I will repeat the fact that of all the people I have met over the years, the happiest are those who enjoy outdoor activities, the people who get out of their house. I use the phrase *outdoor activities* very broadly to mean not only true outdoors but also those activities that are out of the house. It can include short road trips, bowling, a softball tournament, an exercise routine, or even bingo on Friday nights. Above all, the longer you feel and act youthful, the better your quality of life and the happier you'll be. I have never met a person over fifty who plays in an adult baseball league, bowling league, tennis league, or any other club who didn't tell me that it added greatly to their life. The personal and social interaction in a common area of interest made them feel more youthful and happier. A critical element to happiness is to get out of the house as much as you can, especially if it is joining with any type of social group.

In terms of physical health, research shows that you live the healthiest life when you include a routine with regular exercise. By regular exercise, I mean we are told by experts to include a regimen of exercise that includes at least twenty minutes a day for three days a week. This should be a lifetime goal, and because it is a lifetime goal, it does not mean we should start when we feel the effects of ill health. Quite the opposite: we should do it to prevent the effects of ill health. That means we don't start at some milestone of thirty years of age, forty, or fifty. We start as young as possible. But if you haven't started, no matter your age, you should start as soon as possible. And by *as soon as possible* I mean today. Taking that first step matters. It's all about taking that first step. Thus a family that understands the critical elements should include an exercise routine with their children to teach their children the benefit of a healthy routine as a way to a happier life. If the children are school-aged, they may get an exercise regimen while in school. But during school vacations or breaks, the family exercise routine should be added. Again, the goal of every parent is to have their children to live a happier life. Including physical activities as a family is a great benefit to your children. As a parent, even a simple routine would be to walk with your children three times a week for twenty minutes each. Think of all the benefits you will gain. You are teaching your children a lifetime skill for a healthy life by showing them that exercise is important to you. You can use the time during your physical exercise routine to teach your children other important life skills. You now have a commitment to spend at least twenty minutes a day with your children; think of all the conversations you can share or lessons you can impart during this dedicated time period. That twenty minutes now allows you to meet your neighbors. That twenty minutes now gives you the opportunity to discuss important issues one-on-one. That twenty minutes allows you learn when something is wrong so you can take proper measures. When you take that walk, I would love to see you wear a bright yellow shirt that reads "I know the Critical Elements of Happiness." It will make others wonder what the critical elements are and hopefully encourage them to ask questions and learn the critical elements to make for a better world.

Your physical exercise can certainly maintain a consistent routine, but I prefer changing my routines and setting goals. These goals can depend on when you started your routine and depending on your age. You can decide what is correct for you. If you want to be more social, I encourage you to look into the various events all around the country. Do a triathlon, a bike race, a 10K run, a 5K canoe trip, or even a 1K walk. Perhaps you could set a goal of increasing your walking distance or speed every day for the next thirty days. It does not matter if you don't finish as long as you don't quit. What matters is if you don't start. Exercise creates a positive attitude. You look better. You feel better. You're healthier. It also results in you eating wiser. Studies have shown that your desire for unhealthy foods will change. You will not see top athletes desiring full-calorie sodas during training. And when you are performing this physical exercise, you can take the opportunity to learn something at the same time. Jog with a headset and download an educational topic. In addition, exercise is a great way to settle your mind if you are angry, upset, or anxious. Try to remain angry for thirty minutes while running. It's essentially impossible to do.

Chapter Ten

Compartmentalization

A CRITICAL ELEMENT TO BEING happy is not just seeking things you love in life but also reducing the negatives. Notice that I used the term *reducing* because it is impossible to eliminate the negatives altogether. In fact there are times in our lives that we all have "healthy" negative feelings we need to feel. It is healthy to feel pain with the loss of a loved one, the end of a relationship, or the loss of income. An initial question is, "What is a negative?" Many are what we perceive. Is the ending of a relationship that was harmful to begin with a negative? No. It is a new beginning. It is an opportunity. Is a flat tire a negative? To some degree it certainly could be, but it also may not be. What if that flat tire happened while parked in your driveway instead of at high speed on a highway while it was raining heavily? What if that flat tire was discovered by you at a slow speed while shopping around town instead of with your unexperienced child driving at high speed? What if that flat tire prevented you from being in an accident on the highway due to your delay? What if, because of your flat tire, a good Samaritan comes to help you, a conversation develops, and you learn something that brings you happiness? Perhaps he offers you a job. Perhaps you are meant to meet him so you can help his family. Perhaps he asks you to join a local baseball team.

The point I am making is that there are many "negative" things in our lives that are truly a matter of perception. The prior examples are totally different scenarios than a situation wherein because of your flat tire, you pull off the road, another driver who is not paying attention plows into your car, and lives are lost. That is clearly a tragedy and truly a negative. If you compare this tragedy to the prior scenarios, you should feel foolish to even consider any of the prior scenarios as negative. To live a happier life, you must learn to see life as a gift and realize that these rough pebbles are just that—pebbles. They are not roadblocks. They are not tragic. Pebbles are easily forgotten or tossed aside and should be considered merely part of living. They should not be considered negative. You must understand that if you allow these minor pebbles to add up, you are harming yourself, and perhaps others around you, if they result in you getting angry or frustrated. I assure you that life will have you run out of toothpaste, get stuck in traffic, have your flight canceled, have a neighbor's dog bark at night, or have a rock crack your windshield. But think how meaningless these events are compared to truly tragic events.

The goal for a happier life is to get rid of the negatives in your life and seek happiness by understanding that being negative harms only you. I will repeat that: being negative harms only you. Do not focus on living your life by looking only forward or backward, but if you must choose one, choose looking forward. I clearly understand that in life, this is not always easily done. Sometimes life can get extremely complicated, such as by a divorce or by a tragic event that causes some type of injury. In the divorce example, even with the legal proceedings being behind you, you may still have alimony payments each month that are a constant reminder. That negative harms only you. Figure out a system to remove those thoughts from your life. Perhaps you pretend those monthly payments are part of a credit card payment. Understand that there is no benefit to you getting angered each time you make that payment. Perhaps you could take steps so the payment is automatically withdrawn, and at least you don't actually have to make the actual transfer each month.

In order to live the happiest life, you will need to learn what I refer to as compartmentalization for those events that are truly negative in your life. What does that mean? It means you practice a technique of separating your emotions to benefit your current circumstances. In general, it means becoming an expert at not looking backward at anything negative. It also helps you to stop worrying especially about things outside your control. Even a Greek philosopher who lived over two thousand years ago realized that "there is only one way to happiness and that is to cease worrying about things which are beyond the power of our will."

In the simplest example of compartmentalization, Have you ever seen a really scary movie at night and then stepped out of the dark theater, as soon as the movie ended, into a dark parking lot? What were your immediate thoughts as you stepped out of the theater and into that dark parking lot? Did you have to think to yourself that it was just a movie and that you need to forget about those flesh-eating zombies? What if you had seen a really funny comedy movie instead of that horror movie? Would you feel differently as you left the theater and stepped into the dark parking lot? In both instances you were doing the exact same thing. You watched a movie then immediately left that theater and stepped into a dark parking lot. It was only your experience in that movie that effected your mental state which in turn effected your perceptions. When you left that happy comedy movie you didn't have to adjust your perceptions. You were happy. But when you left that horror movie you had to take additional mental steps to remind yourself that what you saw in that horror movie was behind you. Maybe I could say that a better way. What you saw in that horror movie was not real. That was a form of compartmentalization. There was no benefit to thinking about those creepy characters in the horror movie. Well, at least until you got into the safety of your car. Then you could scare you sister or girlfriend or maybe your brother with a re-enactment.

Let me give you some additional examples. Let's say that you have the amazing gift of being a pediatric surgeon. When I say amazing gift, I am not just referring to the knowledge of medicine and skilled hands of a surgeon. I am more focused on the inner kindness, the inner beauty and hope you must possess, and the belief you must maintain to save a child. I find it unfathomable to imagine stepping into that doctor's shoes. A pediatric surgeon treats children from the newborn stage through late adolescence. They choose to make pediatric care the core of their medical practice. Your expertise is operating on infants. You have met the parents, and perhaps the siblings, of the child you are about to operate on. They are an amazing family. You could not admire them more. There is nothing more valuable to those parents than their children, and there is a very special place in their hearts reserved for this sick child. You perform the surgery and lose the child. It is beyond your control. Imagine being that doctor having to tell the parents that their child did not live through the surgery. While keeping that thought of that painful experience, there is something additional that you have to understand. The doctor also has a family. He has children. And the doctor is now needing to go home to celebrate a birthday of one of his children. His child is unaware of what this amazing doctor just went through. To this child, he is just Dad. Dad has to be an expert in separating this birthday from the surgery. But no one, no matter your experience, can simply set aside or forget the loss of a child. This doctor, who is just Dad to his own child, knows that the family who lost a child will be grieving immeasurably from the loss of the child. Yet at the same time, he has to be Dad, hug his child, and play the role that includes acting like a kid. And Dad must do that to remain healthy, and he is only able to do that because he did his best. He has to not look backward. That is compartmentalization. As a doctor, he realizes that he has the ability to save a lot more children even though he knows the risk of a loss remains in the future. Compartmentalization is the understanding that looking backward and holding on to things that are truly negative can only be harmful. In fact, it can become paralyzing.

Let me give you another example of compartmentalization. We can likely agree that the day of an IRS audit is not going to be an amazing day. And how about the days that precede the day of the audit? Is there a benefit to worrying? No. As I stated earlier in this book, as an absolute statement, there is no benefit to worrying. Let's say that you have an important business presentation that you need to give the day before the audit. You need to be focused. Is there any benefit about worrying about the audit? No. By mentally setting aside the audit, by compartmentalizing, you will not ruin the day before the audit or any other day. Simply approach the audit as any other bridge you have to cross. And don't ruin that part of the day after you walk out of the audit.

Another example is a story involving a car full of adults and children on their way to a holiday family gathering. They just brought the car in for service because they heard a funny noise and knew they were going on this road trip and wanted a safe trip with a dependable vehicle. The dealer told them it was a faulty transmission issue and after a huge service bill they get the car back ahead of the journey. They had travelled less than half the journey when the car, after making that noise again, fails along the route. The local dealer is closed and the kids are cold and yelling. At great expense they have to have the car towed and get a rental vehicle. None of which they can afford, especially after the huge dealer bill. Is there a benefit for an adult to scream at their children to stop yelling? Is there a benefit to being upset with the dealer? This is actually a perfect opportunity to teach your children about compartmentalization. This whole episode has to be put behind all of you in order to enjoy the family gathering. A parent who understands the critical elements also understands that everyone is actually safe. That is a very good thing. The breakdown of the vehicle was not in the middle lane of a high-speed highway. The only thing lost is some extra travel time and the expense associated with the breakdown which they can address later with the dealer. Do not let this encounter ruin the family getaway and family gathering. If they compartmentalize their understandable frustration they will clearly benefit. If they choose to stay angered and frustrated they can harm each of themselves, their family and their extended family. They need to put it behind them. They need to arrive at the family gathering as though they never had car trouble. That is compartmentalization.

You may ask, "How exactly does one put the negative out of their mind? How do you compartmentalize?" There are likely many books written on this single subject. You can choose a method that is best for you. Quite honestly, I have never read one. I simply learned what works for me by trial and error. There are mental steps you can take as well as physical steps you can take. I addressed some of the physical steps you can take in prior chapter 9 when I mentioned it's hard to stay angry when you're exercising hard. I had noted that it is difficult to remain angry for thirty minutes while running. But another example of a physical step or system to compartmentalize is to use your phone. When you are frustrated, sad or angered by something you need to focus your mind on something else. That *something else* can be an app on your phone that can bring a smile back. Pick an app that will keep your mind busy and also add sounds that you enjoy. In this manner your sense of sight and sense of hearing are both occupied. Do this long enough to calm your mind. You can also use your phone to call a friend or someone from your core of support. You can tell your friend about what is bothering you if you are seeking help or advice and you are truly willing to listen. But I would strongly suggest not doing this. A better phone call would be to not tell your friend what is bothering you but to instead pick a topic that is positive to chat about. After all, your friend cannot stop your anger, sadness or frustration, only you can.

Let me also give you some mental steps that work for me. For example, sometimes I simply say out loud, "There is no benefit for me to think of that right now," and I begin to focus on what I need to focus on. If the negative thoughts pop back in, I repeat the statement and refocus on what I am working on. Notice that I stated that I focus on something else. Preferably it is something that takes concentration. If your mind is idle, anything can creep back into it. Another method you can use is to imagine yourself alone or with someone you trust the most. You can do this no matter what is around you, but it is best if things are quiet around you. For example, you could be on a busy subway car with lots of noise and people around you, but close your eyes. If you choose this method, mentally picture yourself in a quiet, peaceful place that you truly enjoy. To keep your mind busy, you want to add things to that peaceful place. Try to pick a peaceful place that you have actually visited to make the mental picture easier to establish; perhaps it is the middle of an open field, or the isolated ledge on a mountain path. You can picture yourself in a rowboat in the middle of a calm lake on a sunny day. It is a big lake, and you are in the center. You begin to add elements to this mental picture to keep your mind busy. You can see the shore all around you, with a slight breeze moving the trees. You can hear a fish splash in the distance. As you concentrate on the beauty of that lake and the other elements around you, that car failure or IRS audit will fade away. To make things easier, I suggest putting any physical reminder such as that IRS audit notice in a place out of your view before you picture yourself on that lake. That way when you open your eyes, you have no reason to think about it. Simply focus on that family gathering or enjoying that concert with that special someone (a scenario from chapter 1).

A fourth example of compartmentalization is the big game. A player who exceeds in golf, football, tennis, bowling, baseball, or volleyball is bound to practice compartmentalization whether they realize it or not. Let's pick the sport of golf. If you are in a tournament on the last day, and you hit an errant tee shot, what is the benefit of having your emotions frustrate you? None. I mentioned earlier in this book that if you don't have principles, then you stand for nothing. When I say principle, I mean a true belief. One of the principles of a winner should be the understanding of how fortunate they are. Although it took a lot of tremendously hard work to get to that level, there still must be a true understanding that one is still fortunate. In fact, that understanding and belief will make you a happier person. One side of that belief is the understanding that all could instantly change tomorrow. As I said, if you take things for granted, you will appreciate them less. Conversely, the more you appreciate, the happier you will be. One's future can change quickly. Although I am certainly not a negative person, I can easily come up with examples that can change anyone's life almost instantly. Being struck by lightning, losing a child, being involved in a car crash, or experiencing a life-changing injury. Thus someone with the knowledge of the critical elements appreciates that the life we experience every day in good health is a gift. A golfer who hit the errant shot should be thinking only about the errant shot in terms of improving his next shot. At the same time, and more importantly, that player should be thinking how fortunate they are to be in this setting and playing at this level. Imagine if the worst thing that happened to you in life is that you placed fourth instead of first in the tournament. Do you realize how many people in the world would love to be playing at that level and be in that tournament? The player is going to get old one day. As an old man, he will also look back at films and say that he would love to be playing at that level again.

As a competitor, I also understand the desire to win. But that desire to win the game can also adversely affect your performance. I have never consulted with a professional golfer or any athlete, but if I did, I would say that you should, at every tournament, take a moment to be thankful for what you are experiencing in your life at this time. Do not simply be thankful about being in the tournament. Also be thankful about your family and your friends. If you are wise enough to take that pause, to see that perspective, you will be happier and will be able to perform at your best. That moment of pause is a measure of compartmentalization. You are taking yourself out of the moment to focus on the gifts of the day. Life is not about winning. It is about happiness and the pleasures we enjoy. If winning is the focus, then that golfer will also fully understand something I quoted from chapter 1: "A person who understands the critical elements of happiness also understands that failure and mistakes are a part of life." I certainly applaud that desire to win. That should be fundamental to all of us, but not to a level where it ruins what you love most about the game. Unless that shot provided the golfer with something to learn from, it should be forgotten. Refocus on the next shot and move forward. In fact, I would also say to refocus on the beauty of the course and the gift of playing on that day. If you have lost the love of the game, then you have to ask yourself why. What is going to replace that happiness? Whatever sport you are in, you will realize that as you progress in the sport, that practicing a measure of compartmentalization will be beneficial to you.

It is unfortunate that for most people, one bad day can pull them down much quicker and longer than one great day can keep them up. Don't let it. Sometimes in life, the answer will be no. When things have gone wrong, as they are apt to do, I sometimes smile when I think of a saying by Honore De Balzac: "Hope is a light diet, but very stimulating." It means when things are really bad, the positive thinking of hope can lighten the burden. You simply hope it gets a lot better quickly!

This chapter is meant to teach that many of the things in life you thought were negatives are actually minor and perhaps not even negative in the grand scope of things. Learn and practice to not let the minor things harm your day in any manner. But if you should have a tragic experience, you must learn to compartmentalize those thoughts. Just like anger, envy, worry, or guilt, the effects of a tragic experience are worse if you choose to allow them into your thoughts. Even if the tragic experience was your fault, forgive yourself and move on. If you experienced a tragic loss by the actions of someone else you must try to forgive that individual. Holding that hate inside you will only harm you as discussed in prior chapter 3. Contribute to the happiness of others by being happy yourself. There is a line in *The Sound of Music* song "Something Good" that says, "So somewhere in my wicked, miserable past there must have been a moment of truth." Everyone deserves a second chance. Everyone deserves an opportunity to make things right. Everyone deserves happiness.

Chapter Eleven
Wealth

IMAGINE TWO PICTURES. THE FIRST is of a man standing in front of a beautiful house with an expensive car in the driveway. However, he is standing alone. His drive to earn the highest income came at a cost of never gaining any true friends and being isolated from a family he never spent much time with. The second picture is of a man sitting on a bench with a woman holding his hand sitting next to him, and her head is on his shoulder. Two children are sitting on the ground in front of the bench. The home is clearly mediocre and located in the city, and the car in the driveway is an older model Jeep. The question is not why a Jeep and not a Ford. The question is, Which man is richer? The true fact is that you can have it all when you don't have much.

Does financial wealth determine happiness? Financial security is honestly a factor as one becomes an adult. But does that mean that more wealth means more happiness? Is someone earning $180,000 happier than someone earning $75,000? Is that person happier than someone earning $30,000? In fact it would not take you long to search on the Internet and find stories where the lottery winner's life was ruined once they received the winnings. That money can actually be a mechanism to divide friends and family instead of bring them together. I can give you objective evidence of this by simply going to any local family court and watching the arguments between family members over an estate of any value. Money can be very divisive.

I put this topic of wealth in one of the last chapters because financial wealth is not a litmus test of happiness. But I will say that education is a critical element of happiness. A strong education, both academic and through life experiences, will lead you to financial security. That is because an educated person is in need in every industry and across all sectors of society. Education leads to the freedom to spend your life with passion. It might be the passion of your work. It may be the passion of your family. It may be the passion to learn something new. It may be the passion to try something new. The more experiences you have and the better education you have, the more happiness you are likely to find.

Although this book is not directly about financial success, there is a need to be financially responsible. Being financially responsible has a synergistic benefit should you follow the overall guidance of what I convey. I look at the lessons of this book as an analogy to a person who just lost one hundred pounds after reading a book that was focused on healthy diet and exercise. Yes, the specifics of the healthy diet book resulted in the weight loss, but the synergistic benefits due to the loss of the weight can be amazing. I have never met anyone who lost a great amount of weight and said that losing that weight did nothing else. They always say quite the opposite. By losing the weight, they now have more energy and more confidence, and they are more comfortable in public situations. They now easily fit into airplane seats, and stairs are now motivational instead of an obstacle. This book will hopefully have the same outcome for you. I hope this book leads to a measure of happiness that is far beyond what you expected. But to have that outcome, you have to choose a new path. I want you to find your new path, and that new path is not leading to a specific thing. It is in fact the journey on the new path that you will find exciting and likely leading to other paths you would have never considered in the past. I can tell you that following the lessons of book will factually lead to a much happier path. But you have to choose to make that change, start on that path, and stay on that path.

Let's say you choose to ignore what I just said and rely on your sports skills. Sports Illustrated once estimated that 78 percent of NFL players are either bankrupt or under financial stress within two years of retirement. It also estimated that 60 percent of NBA players are broke within five years of leaving the sport. Why is that? It is simple: they lived beyond their means. Whether you're a professional sports player or a person earning a very honorable living in retail, you must live within your means. Instead of living in a nice home and saving their money, these sports professionals bought large homes with higher real estate taxes, higher utility bills, and higher repair and maintenance costs. They also purchased expensive cars. And why did they do that? Did they truly need those expensive cars, or did they merely want them? And why did they want them? Did they want them because their "friends" or team members had purchased expensive cars? Do you really think that the player's mom, a person who loves her son no matter what, cares what car he drives? She was already immensely proud of what he had accomplished. She could care less about the value of his car. Does a true friend or person who loves you care how big your house is? Do they care what type of car you drive? Does Warren Buffet, a multibillionaire and one of the wealthiest people on the planet, live in a mansion? No. He lives in a home in Nebraska in a house he purchased in 1958 for $31,500. Why? Because he is well educated and knows what he needs. And there is one thing he knows for certain: he does not need to impress others. My hope is that by reading this entire book, you will understand those same facts. The professional sports players were likely trying to impress others or were seduced by the glamorous marketing of products. When each of these players went bankrupt or lost their houses, did these "friends" rush to help? Did any of those folks help them financially? Likely not. In the end, comments from your enemies may hurt, however the hurt from friends not standing by and supporting you is forever remembered.

So in the end, they were false friends. Keep that in mind when you are trying to impress others. That is not what brings happiness.

Then why were these players trying to impress others in the first place? Is that where happiness is found? Of course not. This lesson is one I stated earlier in this book. Do not make a purchase simply because you think it will make you look more important or desirable to other people. You should make a purchase based only on how it makes you feel personally and what you need. I also stated in chapter 1 that the most critical element of the critical elements is to learn to recognize those who truly care for you in life. They are your core of support and will likely be with you for most of your life. Those who care about you most don't care about the car you drive or the street you live on, except to hope that you are safe. If you are spending money to impress someone you wish to date, then you are already on a path to a failed relationship.

With slight exceptions like winning the lottery, dreams don't work unless you do. But work can be very rewarding, interesting, exciting, and even fun. It can be something you actually desire, as I do. Work is not a bad word. I find it something I very much look forward to. I was taught a lesson by my grandfather, who never went to college, that the only thing in life achieved without effort is failure. I am not one who believes in destiny, unless destiny means a lot of hard work. By just sitting on a couch, the phone is not suddenly going to ring with a job offer. It takes hard work to accomplish things you believe in. If you don't have a passion to lead you in a direction, that is okay. When it comes to earning money, find out what you're really good at and do that. You should try to be good at two or more things in life for greater financial security. You can be a really good painter, but then you need to be good with people so others will work for you. You also have to be good with billing and communicating with customers, or have someone on staff who is.

Although this is a book about happiness, I will touch upon a fundamental lesson to gaining wealth. You must learn the difference between an asset and a liability. An asset earns money for you, whereas a liability takes money out of your pocket. If you have money to save and invest by spending your money wisely, then buy assets that go up in value. Not all investments such as real estate, stocks, and bonds go up in value. Invest in areas in which you have knowledge. Do not invest because some so-called expect tells you it's a great place to invest. Invest in what you know, and nothing more. There is a great saying by William Hazlitt: "Prosperity is a great teacher; adversity is greater." Having nothing truly helps you to appreciate when you've earned something. Both of these statements do not relate only to financial independence or wealth, gained by hard work. This is also true of struggling to get the best education and having difficulty in trying to learn to play a musical instrument. You will appreciate those things more because you had to work hard to achieve them.

There is an adage that says knowledge is power and success depends on how much a person knows. I certainly agree that knowledge is a critical element to happiness because it offers opportunities that are not available without it. But knowledge without action can be useless. Professors and academics of the world, in spite of possessing a great deal of education and knowledge, are not the millionaires of today's world. You also see people like Steve Jobs, who, in spite of dropping out of college, was highly successful in life. Henry Ford, inventor of the automobile and the founder of the Ford Motor Company, had only a few years of schooling. How did these men become successful and do better than other educated men of their time? Because they had an overwhelming passion for something. They had a vision at making something better and were driven to make that vision a reality. There are only really three reasons why you can fail in life. One is lacking knowledge. The second is that, even with the knowledge, you are not motivated to act. The third is making bad decisions. If you seek knowledge and are driven to act, then the third reason for failure is overcome with experience. We have all made some bad decisions, but we can learn from them. When you learn from them, you eliminate the third reason for making bad decisions.

Notice that I said only three reasons. That is an absolute statement, meaning people who blame others for not succeeding are being dishonest with themselves. Let's assume the reason you say you are not successful today is because of the school you went to, the neighborhood you lived in, the poor diet you ate, or your older brother beat you up every day. The list could go on and on. How do any of those factors, even if true, change anything? They can slow you down but certainly not stop you from being whoever you wish to be. Again, seek the greatest knowledge, be self-motivated to succeed in whatever you do, and start to apply yourself in a career path. The past is the past however you perceive it, but it is still the past. Stop living in that past and those excuses. Your future, with great happiness, is in front of you.

Another important point to make, is that just because someone has wealth, that does not mean they have knowledge. Knowledge can lead to wealth, but it does not mean the converse is true. It does not mean that those with great wealth have great knowledge. Most everyone in the world has knowledge limited to the field of their expertise. Do not listen to someone just because they have wealth. That is not the litmus test of knowledge. Wealth can be gained in numerous ways. Wealth may have been obtained by being a great songwriter, a successful novelist, a great athlete, or even an internet sensation for doing really stupid things with lots of followers. Perhaps the money was inherited, or perhaps it was attained through illegal means. Whatever the case, the amount that someone has in personal wealth does not mean they are someone you should listen to, and it certainly does not mean they are someone you should automatically trust. As I said in chapter 1, you should trust only those who are in your core of support. Do not listen to some wealthy person or someone with fame who tries to sway you into voting for someone or investing in something because they supposedly know more than you do. Likely they do not. Having money is not some magical field of expertise.

There are other folks who combine their passion to help others, which results in certain career paths. These are amazing people because these careers can be quite difficult. Why do folks want to be firefighters? It is certainly not because they want to run into environments that could kill them. Why do folks want to help the homeless? That is a very difficult career that brings individuals in personal crisis to your door. They do so because of those times when everything goes very right. When they have that day of success and excitement, when everything goes right, we hope all those difficult times are outweighed by the reward. Those are people who understand what it takes to give on a daily basis.

Because this is a book about happiness, I try to also teach reducing the negatives. I strongly advise that you never invest in a friend's or family member's business unless that money is literally a gift with no expected return. Even if you are an expert in that business, you cannot be certain that the person running the business will listen to your advice. That is not happiness. It will be frustrating if you see the person who is running the business not put in the time to make it a success. That is not happiness. I also strongly advise parents to have discussions with their children about their estates. I have seen firsthand families torn apart, never to speak to each other again, over the divestment of an estate. Parents think it is a good thing to leave money to their children, only to have their children fight over the money or the assets.

What is most important is that whatever your standard of living, you should avoid living beyond it. It would be difficult to experience the happiness in life with the burden and stress of being behind in your payments. Studies show a link between financial worries and mental health problems such as depression, anxiety, and substance abuse. Financial problems adversely impact your mental health and your physical health. Thus, a critical element of happiness is to live within your means. If you have read this entire book, you have learned to not spend money to impress others, and to seek the highest education to gain the greatest opportunities to earn.

There is an old proverb accredited to Confucius that reads, "The man who moves a mountain begins by carrying away small stones." I hope this book and the small stones I've uncovered help to change your life in momentous ways.

Chapter Twelve

Being Honest with Yourself, and
Other Matters to Consider

IT IS NOT UNCOMMON TO see a news story where someone says the day's events make them look at life differently, and they are now more thankful. That is another way of saying they took a lot of things for granted. After seeing those news clips, I wonder why these people waited. Why was a tragic loss or tragic event or harrowing experience required to appreciate life more? Can we learn to be happier or merely choose to be happier? My objective answer is yes. But is it as simple as saying, "Today, I'm going to start with a fresh outlook and see my life differently"? These people in the news event claim to now be living life to the fullest. If I asked them to prove that to me, what would be their answer? What evidence could they give me? What evidence can you give me to objectively prove that you are living life to the fullest? I don't think living life to the fullest is the best way to live if it means pushing your limits. Is life better going the fastest on a motorcycle? Is that happiness? I have learned that even though many people say they have changed, most people are set in their ways and don't actually change. You can be that exception given the proper knowledge. You can be that exception if you practice all the elements of this book. Exactly what changes are you going to make?

People don't generally change overnight. If someone hates dogs, they will not suddenly change. If someone has a negative opinion of you, ignore it and realize they will likely not change. Trust that the person is not your friend and move on. Pick a new friend from the billions of other people on the planet. Get away from that person. In fact, get that person totally out of your life. A good measure in life is to frequently ask yourself these three questions. Don't wait until you are about to die to ask at least these questions! The first question is, Did you have (or are you having) a wonderful life? The second is, Are you responsible for making at least five other people's days better this week with acts of kindness? And the third is, Will this make your life happier to such a degree that you might even remember it on your last day? I have never met anyone who looked back at life and said they were really proud that they had made all their mortgage payments on time.

The first question is actually a very broad question and thus has many elements to it. Did you have an intense love and true friends? Did you find passions (note the plural) in life? Did you find your work rewarding? Did you seek new adventures and reach new goals? Did you try to act young as long as you could? If you can answer *yes* to this first question relatively quickly, that is a very good sign because your perception is what is important. If not, it's time to get on a new path. The second question is more specific. Are you the type of person who reaches out to help others because you understand what you get in return? You might get a smile or a thank-you, but that is not why good people help each other. We help other people because it is the right thing to do. Being kind to others is reward in and of itself. And if you answered *no* to the second question, you should ask yourself why and make an effort to treat others better. Open that door for a stranger. Find the owner of the pet. Help jump-start that car with a dead battery. Offer kind words to the person who is sad. Send a handwritten note to an old friend. Call your mom. The third question is about the present. "Will this picnic, this bike ride, this movie, or this job make my life happier? Do I enjoy what I am doing and who I am doing it with?" If not, you need to get on a different path and change things.

Everyone wants to be appreciated, and people like being around others who show appreciation. If you help someone, and they merely say a simple thank-you, should you truly feel appreciated? That is a difficult question to answer because a large portion of society uses the phrase "thank you" without any emotion behind it. You should not be like everyone else. You should choose to make those who help you understand that you truly do appreciate their help. No matter how minor the assistance, be sure to communicate more than just a thank-you. For example, you can say, "Thank you for holding the door open for me. You are very kind." You can also say, "Thank you for holding the door for me. I am fortunate that you were here to help." If you are stranded on the side of the road, and someone stops to change your tire, is a simple thank-you enough? At the very least, you should get their address so you can send them a thank-you note. It would be even better if, during the time they change your tire, you can find out if they like coffee or favor a certain restaurant. If so, get a gift card for coffee or for their favorite restaurant and mail it to them. You will find amazing people out there who don't want to give out their mailing address because they want nothing in return. They are acting out of true kindness and not for personal gain. Those are the exact people you want to reward. Try to get their email. With today's technology, you can send them an electronic gift card with a message attached.

Don't ignore fear, but don't let it rule you. Face up to it. Return that phone call about the late payment. A lot about achieving happiness is also about balance. Every day will not be perfect; that is just life. You have to understand that all of us experience failure throughout our lives. The question is, How will it affect you? Failure is not a bad thing. It means that at least you tried. For example, let's say you are a student athlete, and you lose a wrestling match in front of your entire class. Is that failing? Absolutely not. Anyone who says anything negative to you about your loss is not a friend. I can state with certainty that trying and failing is a lot better than never trying. When people show you their true colors by being derogatory to you, that is not a bad thing. It simply means you now know that you cannot trust them to be friends. Knowing good people from bad people is important in life. Don't let anyone tell you differently.

During a tournament, a golfer may focus on a particular part of his swing when using his short irons because he knows his weakness. The golf swing is very complex and can be broken down into elements. Therefore, you cannot simply think, "Do a good swing." Knowing your weaknesses is a good thing. Having weaknesses is not a bad thing. One form of weakness is when you know you cannot do without something or, more important, someone. And needing someone can be a very good thing. But first you have to admit that you need someone for it to be actually a great thing. As I mentioned earlier in this book, we all need others. Let's assume you admit to someone that you need them. That is certainly something very important and caring to tell a parent. But let's also assume that this person you need is actually someone you realize you love. That could feel amazingly exciting. My advice is always to share that excitement with that person. Do not worry that this person might not feel the same way. Do not filter your true feelings from those you can truly trust. That said, what if this person is not in love with you, or falls out of love with you in time? Then any feelings of regret due to the ending of that relationship should be set aside. You clearly had time together that made you feel amazing. Be happy for those moments and seek more with a new beginning. Again, do not look backward. Things like envy, worry, panic, anxiety, sorrow, resentment, and regret harm only you. Your life is in front of you, not behind you. Imagine if the golf player was worried about his next shot or angered by his last. What if he was feeling panic as he approached his next shot? Do any of these feelings or emotions benefit the golfer? Even given such a practical example, why would you think that such feelings would not harm you? Why would you ever presume that it wouldn't hurt you in your daily life? Focus on the positive in sports and in life. Not only ignore the negatives but also improve the positives. And take objective steps to make your life better. And put those steps in writing. Perhaps you need to put in place a specific routine that will help you if you ever have such negative feelings. Maybe it includes calling someone. Maybe it includes meditation. Maybe it is getting better at compartmentalization. Maybe it's helping someone else so you can see that your problems are minor compared to others.

If *you* are feeling a little down on a certain day, a great solution may be to ask your partner how can you make *their* day better. Or better yet, if you know what they really like, spend the day putting together a surprise for them to experience. When was the last time you asked your partner, or anyone else, "How can I make your day better?" An amazing day is not something that someone else tells you; it is something you feel. My hope is that by reading this entire book you have learned methods to create those great days, as suggested in chapter 5.

I understand that there is a great number of folks who work for a company not as a passion but for financial security. My hope is that those same folks are striving to better themselves with education at the same time. If I was a company owner, I'd meet with each of my team managers and ask them about each of their employees. As the manager thinks of each employee, I would ask the manager to consider whether she first views the employee very positively, in a mediocre manner, or negatively, and why. I'd ask each manager to provide me with the number of employees that fall into each category. Then I'd likely consider firing the manager who tells me of the greatest number of employees she considers in a negative light. Why? Think of it logically, as I do. Assume that you work in a company of one hundred employees. Now consider a first view where you have a negative opinion of all of those ninety nine other employees. Could you be happy? No. Could you be productive? You definitely would not work to your full potential because you'd tend to limit your communication with fellow employees. A company cannot succeed without communication or motivated employees. Consider another possibility where you respect and enjoy each and every one of those other ninety nine employees. Are you likely to be happy? Yes. Could you be productive? The likelihood is that you would be motivated to be very productive so that the company does well, and you can all be equally rewarded. Positive employees who interact with the other employees get a lot more accomplished. Given these two clearly diverse scenarios, why would I want to retain a manager who keeps a large number of negative employees in the company? What are the odds that the problem is not with the employees but with the manager? If there is an equal number of employees assigned to the staff of each manager, why would there be a great disparity with only one manager? I would suspect that the best manager is going to tell me of the great number of positive employees on her staff and will praise each individually and by name. That is the manager I certainly want to keep.

There is a quote from the movie *Interstellar*, and it comes at a critical phase when a computer states, "It's not possible." the actor replies, "No, it's necessary." This scene occurs when all seems lost, and they were seeking options for the next step. What will you do when you must succeed? You do the impossible. What I am asking you is, What could you accomplish if you had no fear? What if you didn't need to please anyone else? What if you didn't have to worry about what others thought? Would you have tried out for wrestling or tennis in school even though you may lose in front of the entire school but still love the sport? Well, here is something you should already understand from this book. It is a fact that you do not need to please others. This fact can lead to a feeling of freedom and greater happiness. This means you should follow your dreams. You do not need to worry what others think, and you do not need to please anyone else but yourself. Those who truly love you will encourage you to follow your dreams. Live life without limits imposed by others. Being a decision maker is a good thing. Trust your intuition and experience. Sometimes you'll get it wrong, but that is okay. It is better than not deciding. You would not go out for breakfast and tell the waitress that you'll have whatever the person on your right orders. (Although at least you made the decision about the person being on your right!)

Someone who understands the critical elements of happiness is someone who understands how valuable they are, yet they are humble at the same time. They also know they will likely never gain fame, and they will never have their name put on a high school or even a street sign. But they are confident they are a great parent, a great friend, or maybe a great colleague. Not having any public recognition is of no concern because vanity is not a good trait. I will repeat a story of vanity to illustrate what I mean. A stag overpowered by heat came to a spring to drink. Seeing his own shadow reflected in the water, he greatly admired the size and variety of his horns, but he felt angry with himself for having such slender and weak feet. While he was thus contemplating himself, a lion appeared at the pool and crouched to spring upon him. The stag immediately took to flight and exerted his utmost speed. As long as the plain was smooth and open, he kept himself easily at a safe distance from the lion. But upon entering a wooded area, he became entangled by his horns, and the lion quickly came up to him and caught him. When too late, he thus reproached himself: "Woe is me! How I have deceived myself! These feet that would have saved me, I despised, and I gloried in these antlers that have proved my destruction." Don't be flattered by yourself or any part of yourself. Someone who understands the critical elements of happiness will realize that you are the most important person in the world to someone, even if no one else knows it. You may be the most important person in the world while helping a victim out of a burning car. You may be the most important person in the world to your newborn child, who relies upon you for everything. You may be the most important person in the world to your grandmother, who lives alone and whom you visit. You may be the most important person in the world, for even a fleeting moment, when you prevent that person from slipping and hitting their head. Maybe those other people will never understand how important you were to them at those moments. But you should understand that some of the kindest people in the world know—those with the biggest hearts, those who don't care if their names are never on a school. They can see it by your kindness. And if you are a person who understands the critical elements of happiness, you will begin to see those kind people as well. They were always there, just as you were always there for someone. I will keep your secret of being the most important person in the world if you can keep mine.

Chapter Thirteen
An International Movement

AS I STATED IN CHAPTER one of this book my overall goal is to have your life exceed my life in terms of happiness. I dare to imagine how great a world would be if we could objectively have each generation happier than the prior generation. My hope is that those who read this book feel the same way as I do because I cannot make the world a happier place without you. And if you feel this way wouldn't it be great to meet others that feel the same way as us? Isn't there strength in knowing that more and more of us seek nothing more than overall happiness in our lives? We understand that education and hard work are good things. We believe that new experiences, including meeting others, can lead to positive experiences for all of us. We believe in such things as love, hope, serenity, humility, kindness, benevolence, empathy, generosity, truth, compassion and faith. We do not reward negative behavior. We are against envy, greed, arrogance, inferiority, self-pity, resentment, lies, false pride and ego. Why? Because these traits do not lead to happiness. We understand that even small things matter in a good way as well as a bad way. Saying "thank you" with sincerity may seem small but it is in fact very important especially if we multiply that sincere *thank you* by millions of people. Maybe someone witnessing a sincere *thank you* will be encouraged to perform acts of kindness. Think of the alternative where you hear millions of people saying, "shut up" or "stop that". How would that make your day feel? We believe that stealing something even as small as a flower from someone's garden is still stealing and wrong.

As an engineer, what is a simple tool to tell others that you understand the critical elements of happiness? Perhaps one is by your actions. But when I say *tell others* I mean truly meeting them in person where you can say "hello". Virtual meetings will never take the place of a face-to-face meeting. Virtual meetings can certainly be helpful but they are not equivalent to actually meeting. A mom touching her newborn and holding a newborn is not even comparable to seeing a newborn via an on-line camera. A dad reading a bedtime story to his children and tucking them into bed cannot be replaced with a video. A long hug from a best friend who lives far away cannot be replaced with a video conference. Eating a meal alone while talking to someone on a cell phone is still eating alone. Telling someone you are sorry via text or email is not as sincere or meaningful as doing so in person. What is a way to outwardly let others know that we feel the same way? That we'd enjoy meeting them just to chat with no expectations. How can we let someone else know that we'd enjoy a conversation with a kind stranger?

I am proposing an international day, once a year, to wear a yellow hat or perhaps a yellow shirt that reads "The Critical Elements", or, perhaps more generally "Share My Table". I hope that day is my birthday on September 16th of every year. Even though I am living an amazing life it would be even more amazing if I could see others, on my birthday, letting me know that they feel the way I do. And if enough people start wearing yellow on September 16th it will encourage others to ask what it means. That in turn will encourage others to read this book and hopefully impact their lives in a positive manner. It would bring me great joy to know that I may be bringing happiness to others through the help of others. Thus bringing happiness to folks I have never met. That I somehow made a positive difference in someone else's life. Perhaps there are those that want to wear a less-seen yellow wristband every day of the year that reads "critical elements" so as to be more subtle. I also encourage that. Let others outwardly know that you support kindness and reaching out to others.

September 16th is not meant to be a day for volunteerism although it may take that form for some of you if that is what makes you truly happy. Instead it is a day about *your* happiness. Wearing a yellow "The Critical Elements" hat or shirt essentially says that you welcome others to share your table. And although "share your table" does not only mean literally eating a meal together it certainly could. It means we all understand that life can be difficult at times and sharing a friendly conversation can be rewarding for all of us. The meaning of "share my table" is an admission that you, or we, don't like eating alone. We understand that spending time together, not in some hurried manner, is a good thing. Since the statement "share my table" actually includes sharing a meal together, wouldn't it be nice to actually go into a restaurant and share a table? If you go into a restaurant and see a "The Critical Elements" shirt you should ask that person to share your table. Wouldn't it be nice to share a meal to learn if they are a teacher or perhaps a student or perhaps a doctor with everyone understanding that we all pay for our own meals? Wouldn't it be nice to meet someone in a store or in the park or on the sidewalk and not be afraid to immediately start up a conversation about their children or their pets? Perhaps you'll chat about where they have travelled or what languages they speak. Perhaps you'll share each other's most embarrassing moments. Perhaps you'll learn about each other's current passions. Perhaps you will learn that this person is a martial arts expert and you are introduced to this interest for the first time. Perhaps a child in one family will ask an older couple in another family how they met. Perhaps you meet an astronaut, a mountain climber, a concert pianist, a plumber, an expert mason or landscaper. Maybe you can ask them what is their favorite movie or favorite book. I hope a few folks reply that this is their favorite book! Perhaps you'll talk about a surprise you gave someone. The list of conversational elements is endless with the focus being on positive conversations and learning about each other. Thus conversations on such things as politics or religion, that can separate people, should be generally avoided.

Perhaps you'll be at an airport waiting for a plane and see someone with the yellow wrist band. That is a sign that they welcome a nice conversation. Perhaps you just joined a sports team and you don't feel comfortable reaching out to others. Then you see one of your team members with the yellow wrist band and the words "Critical Elements". You know that person likely also believes in hard work and understands the benefit of new experiences such as meeting others. In fact a person who is shy could benefit directly by wearing the wristband since you may be hesitant introducing yourself.

Wouldn't it be nice to simply see other "critical elements" hats to know that you are not alone in the way you think. Wouldn't it be nice to tell others around you, who may feel alone at times, that you want to meet them because it could enrich your life to learn about them? Living a life of solitude cannot compare to a life full of positive relationships.

In completing this book I hope you have fully come to understand that you are a critical element to someone else and for someone else. And a part of true happiness is learning to love like you have never loved before.

David Andrew can be reached via
david@thecriticalelements.com.

CPSIA information can be obtained
at www.ICGtesting.com
Printed in the USA
LVHW040919170322
713543LV00002B/52